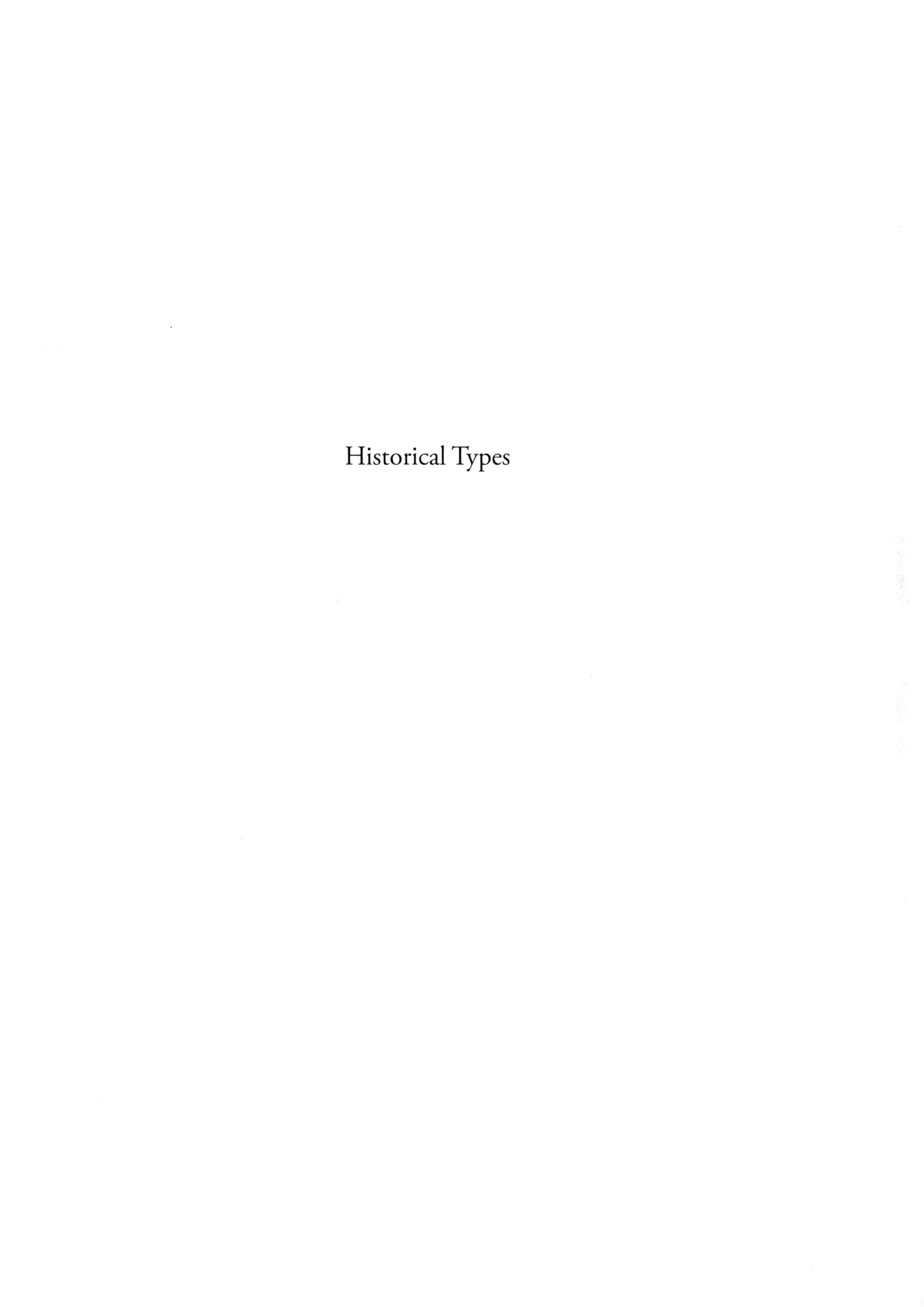

Historical Types

Frontispiece The genial punchcutter, Johann Michael Fleischman, surrounded by the tools of his trade.
Illustration from the *Proef den letteren* of Johann Enschedé, published in 1768 (see also *E2*).
Chicago, The Newberry Library, Case Wing z 40546 .2642.

Historical Types

FROM GUTENBERG TO ASHENDENE

Stan Knight

Oak Knoll Press
New Castle, Delaware
2012

First Edition 2012

Published by

Oak Knoll Press
310 Delaware Street
New Castle, Delaware 19720, USA
www.oakknoll.com

ISBN: 978-1-58456-298-6

©2012 Stan Knight. All rights reserved.

Publishing Director: Laura R. Williams

No part of this book may be reproduced in any manner
without the express written consent of the publisher, except in cases
of brief excerpts in critical reviews and articles.
All inquires should be addressed to:
Oak Knoll Press, 310 Delaware Street, New Castle, Delaware 19720.

Printed in the United States of America on acid-free paper meeting the requirements of
ANSI/NISO Z39.48-1992 (Permanence of Paper)

Library of Congress Cataloging-in-Publication Data

Knight, Stan, 1937-
 Historical types : from Gutenberg to Ashendene / Stan Knight. -- First edition.
     pages cm
 Includes bibliographical references and indexes.
 Summary: "A survey of major developments in type design from the fifteen
to the twentieth century, grouped by historical period. Concise commentary
about the type and its maker accompanies three photographs of each type.
Begins with an overview of the history of type and its study"--Provided by
publisher.
 ISBN 978-1-58456-298-6
 1. Type and type-founding--Specimens. 2. Type and type-founding--History.
3. Type designers--Biography. I. Title.
 Z250.K625 2012
 686.2'2--dc23
                    2012028087

Contents

6		Acknowledgements
7		Foreword
8		Introduction

Medieval Types

14	A1	Johann Gutenberg
		Certificate of Indulgence, 1454
16	A2	Johann Gutenberg
		The 42-line Bible, 1455
18	A3	Johann Fust & Peter Schoeffer
		The Mainz Psalter, 1457
20	A4	William Caxton
		The Canterbury Tales, 1476
22	A5	Erhard Ratdolt
		Elementia geometriae, 1482

Italian Renaissance Types

24	B1	Sweynheym & Pannartz
		De divinis institutionibus, 1465
26	B2	Nicolas Jenson
		Epistolae ad Brutum, 1470
28	B3	Aldus Manutius
		De Aetna, 1496
30	B4	Aldus Manutius
		Liber de imaginatione, 1501
32	B5	Francesco Griffo
		Petrarch: Opere, 1503
34	B6	Ludovico degli Arrighi
		De arte poetica, 1527

French Renaissance Types

36	C1	Simon de Colines
		Liber contra gentiles, 1528
38	C2	Robert Estienne I
		Exemplaria literarum, 1537
40	C3	Claude Garamont
		Les vies des hommes illustres, 1559
42	C4	Claude Garamont
		De venatione, 1555
44	C5	Robert Granjon
		Romanae historiae, 1568
46	C6	Robert Granjon
		Livre de perspective, 1560

Baroque Types

48	D1	Jean Jannon
		Espreuves des caractères, 1621
50	D2	Jean Jannon
		Les principaux poincts de la foy, 1642
52	D3	Christoffel van Dijck
		Terence: Comoediae, 1701
54	D4	Christoffel van Dijck
		Terence: Comoediae, 1701
56	D5	Miklós Tótfalusi Kis
		Saggi di naturali esperienze, 1691
58	D6	Miklós Tótfalusi Kis
		Saggi di naturali esperienze, 1691
60	D7	William Caslon I
		Juvenal: Satirae, 1845
62	D8	William Caslon I
		The Diary of Lady Willoughby, 1844

Neoclassical Types

64	E1	Philippe Grandjean
		Médailles de Louis le Grand, 1702
66	E2	Johann Fleischman
		Proef van letteren, 1768
68	E3	Pierre-Simon Fournier
		Les caractères de l'imprimerie, 1764
70	E4	Pierre-Simon Fournier
		Les caractères de l'imprimerie, 1764
72	E5	John Baskerville
		Terence: Comoediae, 1772
74	E6	John Baskerville
		Terence: Comoediae, 1772

Rational Types

76	F1	Firmin Didot
		Virgil: Opera, 1791
78	F2	Giambattista Bodoni
		Horace: Opera, 1791
80	F3	Giambattista Bodoni
		Horace: Opera, 1791

Nineteenth-century Types

82	G1	Richard Austin
		Wilson & Sons Specimen, 1833
84	G2	Robert Besley
		Fann Street Specimen, 1857
86	G3	Alexander Phemister
		Miller & Richard Specimen, 1868

Private Press Types

88	H1	William Morris
		The Earthly Paradise, 1896
90	H2	T J Cobden-Sanderson
		Paradise Lost, 1902
92	H3	C H St John Hornby
		Lo Paradiso, 1905

95		Glossary
98		Select Bibliography
101		Indices

Acknowledgements

Compiling this new, broad survey of historical types would have been impossible without the encouragement, interest, and expert advice of one eminent scholar in particular. I am much indebted to James Mosley, Visiting Professor at the University of Reading; he has been for me with *Historical Types*, what Professor Julian Brown was for me with my earlier work, *Historical Scripts* – a wise counsel and a sure friend. I have especially appreciated his penetratingly incisive comments on my draft texts, even when he needed to tell me that I had got it wrong! In the event, he has saved me from numerous (potentially embarrassing) *faux pas*, but of course, any remaining shortcomings in this work are purely my own responsibility.

I also received generous and valuable assistance from Paul Gehl at The Newberry Library in Chicago. During my study sessions at the Newberry, and in frequent correspondence in-between, Paul has been extremely helpful, giving of his time and attention, far beyond the mere 'call of duty'.

James Clough, teacher of the history and theory of typography at the Polytechnic of Milan (and elsewhere), has been particularly supportive. I have been grateful not only for the unselfish way he has shared his professional knowledge, but also for his exceptional proof-reading skills. I am delighted that he agreed to provide a Foreword for *Historical Types*.

I am indebted to Alastair Johnston who not only allowed me pre-publication view of his ground-breaking study of Richard Austin and his son (see *G1*), but also provided me with much-needed help regarding 19th-century types – even offering to handset some samples for me!

I have also had encouragement and advice from a number of other scholars – Hendrik Vervliet, Robert Bringhurst, Riccardo Olocco, Paul Shaw, and Ewan Clayton among them, for which I am most grateful.

As far back as February 2004, Justin Howes offered to help me to put together a survey of historical type design, which would follow the successful format of *Historical Scripts*. His enthusiasm provided me with the needed impetus, but, sadly, he did not live to see the project even get started.

A mere glance at the Index of Call Numbers in *Historical Types* graphically portrays how much I have relied on the superb collection of The Newberry Library in Chicago for my illustrations. Without that institution, I would have found it practically impossible to have completed this work. It must surely be one of the most extensive resources in North America for the study of printing history, and this book may well be enjoyed as a celebration of that Newberry collection.

The photographer at the Newberry, Catherine Gass, has had the lion's (or lioness') share of the work involved in creating the illustrations for this book, but she has responded enthusiastically to my very particular requests. Her success can be seen in the high quality images shown here.

The digital images from the John Rylands Library in Manchester clearly reveal the dedication to the pursuit of excellence of James Robinson and his staff. He responded to my peculiar and precise image requests with enthusiasm and detailed attention, and he produced images of outstanding clarity and usefulness. Indeed, all the staff at JRL have been very pleasant correspondents, and models of efficiency, promptness, and personal service which certain other libraries would do well to emulate.

I also thank my local librarian, Peggy Buehler in Bonners Ferry, who, time and again, persuaded formidable academic libraries all over the Pacific Northwest to part with their rare and precious volumes. Ah, the magic of inter-library loan!

I am very grateful, once again, to Marcia Friedman for her excellent typographic design. It has been a renewed pleasure to work with her. Marcia's close attention to detail and exacting standards fully complement, and compliment, the classic books of type history shown here.

Finally, my loving appreciation to Denys, my wife, for her constant support of this project and her willingness, over the last three years, to endure much isolation during the long period of intense concentration required to bring this work to a successful conclusion.

Stan Knight

Illustrations are reproduced by kind permission of the following institutions:

Bern, Universitätsbibliothek Bern: C1
The Syndics of Cambridge University Library:
 C5, Back cover
Manchester, The John Rylands Library, The University
 of Manchester: Front cover, Fig. 5,
 A1, A2, A3, A4
Paris, Bibliothèque Mazarine: D1
Parma, Biblioteca Palatina: B4
Urbana-Campaign, The Rare Book and Manuscript Library,
 University of Illinois: D5, D6
Washington DC, Library of Congress: Fig. 4

All other illustrations are from the The Newberry Library, Chicago, and are used by kind permission.

Additional images have been supplied by:
Stan Nelson: Fig. 1
Alastair Johnston: Fig. 2
Riccardo Olocco: B4
James Mosley: Back cover

Foreword

Without any disregard for the highly esteemed dexterity of typefounders, papermakers, compositors and pressmen, let it be said that the skill of the old engravers of type (punchcutters) stands above that of all the other crafts involved in the making of printed books. To some extent we can also say that the punchcutters' art has been handed down to us through revivals of many of the same types that are shown on these pages. Those revivals – or to be more precise, those interpretations – often have the names of the original punchcutters, such as Garamond or Caslon.

Early examples

When we select a 'Garamond' font that we are likely to have in our computer, we can set words in any size, and we can be sure that the contours will be perfectly smooth and details such as serifs will be homogeneous. The mathematical vectors that contain the letterforms of our digital fonts ensure this kind of perfection with a single font design usable at all sizes – which makes a stark contrast with the enlarged specimens that Stan Knight offers us on the pages ahead. The rugged imperfection of contours and details of the enlarged lines of Jenson's roman or the 'De Aetna' roman, to name two noteworthy types, is immediately evident. But when books were printed with those types in the 15th century, in their real sizes (about 15 points), informed people regarded them as masterpieces. Several centuries later, Emery Walker and Stanley Morison were of the same opinion too. The 'imperfections' were of no consequence.

   Nevertheless, the enlarged specimens that follow are extraordinarily useful. They allow a clear understanding of the proportions and shapes of the letters, the distribution of thick and thin strokes, and each letter's spatial relationship with its neighbours. We can see exactly how much interpretation (especially of serifs) was needed for the 20th-century revivals of those types. Furthermore, we can get some idea of the texture of handmade paper – each sheet of which was dampened to give a softer, and therefore more receptive surface for the impression of the inked types. In order to appreciate the readability and the effect of the letters assembled into words, lines, and above all columns, Stan also gives us his selection of typefaces as texts reproduced in their original sizes. A realistic and substantial improvement can be made on that only by visiting a historical library and studying copies of the original books.

Venetian types

In about 1470 in Venice, Jenson must have taken some refined example of humanistic script as a basic model for his 'roman' type. While his uppercase shows some similarity to imperial epigraphic capitals, which were becoming fashionable for inscriptions at that time, he made certain design decisions for lowercase letters. Some of these, together with later modifications introduced by Francesco Griffo (who also worked in Venice), have remained standard to this day. Roman type in its late 15th-century Venetian guise was destined to become Italy's permanent gift to the World.

Apart from the important interval of 'Rational' types during the 18th and 19th centuries, 'Old face' romans of Venetian origin have been in use for half a millennium, and they still abound in today's books.

   Unlike the great Venetian romans, not much design decision-making was required of the punchcutters for making blackletter or gothic types, and these tend to be faithful to their original calligraphic models. But that must not detract from Gutenberg's (or Schoeffer's) geniality in making and setting the textura gothic of the 42-line Bible. Each line is in a perfectly harmonious rhythm of black and white, and an ingenious system for justifying the narrow columns – something the scribe was hardly able to do – continues to be unique in the history of the book.

In continuity

It must be emphasized that this book follows *Historical Scripts* by the same author. If it is not unreasonable to consider type to be the mechanization of script, *Historical Types* is in apt continuity with the earlier book. Although there are some excellent publications on the history of type, their illustrations are inadequate for young people trying to grasp the subtle variations of letterforms. Access to several worthwhile blogs and websites can be had with the click of a mouse, but the best of these tend to be erudite discussions or forums for professionals who already possess knowledge of the history and culture of type. What has been missing until now is a source that shows what we see here: high-quality enlarged images of the most significant types in the history of printing. Stan presents the types in a chronological progression, with the necessary discussions on letterform details as well as circumstantial comments on the work of the individual punchcutters or printers.

   This long-awaited contribution to the culture of type will be fundamental, not only to typographers and graphic designers (both students and professionals), but also to bibliographers and students of the history of the book.

James Clough
Milan, Italy
on the Feast of St Matthias, 2012

Introduction

LETTERPRESS PRINTING

This book is not really about the history of printing. Some aspects of that mechanical process must inevitably be considered; but the primary purpose of *Historical Types* is to show, as clearly as possible, what the classic 'landmark' typefaces actually looked like, and to facilitate an awareness of how the design of printing types changed over time.

Making type

One important thing to remember is that every single historical page shown in this book, from Gutenberg to Ashendene, was printed from individual pieces of metal type. The making of metal type relied a great deal on handcraft skills and required a lot of technical precision.

First, a punch is engraved with the form of the letter in relief at actual size, but reversed left to right (see *Fig. 1*). (Check the actual size of the type illustrated in *B5*, and note that this is by no means the smallest type ever cut.) The form of the letter is achieved by counter-punching, engraving and/or filing the end of a steel bar, which for medium letters, might be 2½ to 3½ inches long and, say, ¼ inch square. Once the letter has been cut satisfactorily, the steel bar is hardened and tempered. It is then struck into a bar of copper to create the indented strike. The strike, when adjusted, forms the matrix which is inserted into an adjustable hand mould, and the individual type cast (also see *Fig. 1*). From this one matrix thousands of 'identical' type letters (sorts) can be produced. (For a fuller explanation of this process see, for example, Warren Chappell, *A Short History of the Printed Word*, chapter III.)

Each sort is then individually picked out from a typecase, assembled into lines of text, locked in a chase, inked by hand, and printed on a handpress (like an Albion). This form of printing, called letterpress, began with the experiments of Johann Gutenberg and was the common trade practice for nearly 500 years.

Some mechanisation of the manufacture of type occurred in the 19th century. David Bruce Jr of New Jersey patented his typecasting machine in 1838, and this was imported into Britain from 1849. In fact, the *Old Style* type of Miller & Richard (see *G3*), and the types for the Private Presses (*H1–H3*) actually had their type cast by machine. But, in all other respects, their type was handmade and hand set in the manner described. Although Linn Boyd Benton invented a mechanical punchcutter in 1884, and the first functional typesetting machine (the Linotype) was built in 1886, no use of them was made by any of the types shown here.

The punchcutter

Perhaps the single most important influence on the design of historical printing types was the work of the punchcutter. The modern concept of the 'type designer' just did not exist in the very early days of printing. Then, the punchcutter *was* the designer, often forming the unique characteristics of the letters in the process of his engraving. And very early in printing history, punchcutting, and even typefounding, became independent occupations.

In one sense, *Historical Types* could well be described as a celebration of the skill and art of the punchcutter. That explains why Johann Fleischman is smiling at us from the Frontispiece, and why the punch of Baskerville's marvellous letter **Q** forms our tailpiece!

THE FORMAT OF THIS BOOK

Historical Types began life as part of my 'Introduction to Typography' course for graphic designers. When exposed to a proper historical perspective, students not only become aware of the origins of modern font designs, but are also able to grasp the subtle differences between one typeface and another. And through this understanding they can develop the skills necessary to use type in their designs in an appropriate, attractive, and more assured manner. In order to provide this historical perspective in a format designed to capture students' interest and imagination, I soon realised the need for a book like this one. None of the existing books on printing history seemed suitable. So this survey follows the format and style of my earlier work, *Historical Scripts*.

Each of the spreads features a single design, identified with an easily recognised eponym – usually the designer, punchcutter, founder, or publisher related to that particular type. For ease of reference, the 40 examples are grouped into eight sections with headings of my own devising. Classification of historical types is notoriously difficult. The traditional system has long since been an anachronism; it makes no sense to go on describing late 18th-century types as 'Modern', and more recent attempts at categorising have degenerated into labels like 'Garaldes' or 'Didones' (nonsense worthy of Edward Lear). My section headings are not intended to be the *definitive* attempt to classify historical typefaces, but are simply offered as a plain and pragmatic ordering of the examples shown.

The selection of historical types has been chosen with a great deal of care. Yet, while this selection is quite comprehensive, I cannot claim that it is 'collectively exhaustive'. Some worthy type designers like Pierre Haultin, Hendrik

Fig. 1 The process of making metal type. From left to right: a steel punch, a copper strike, and a justified matrix of a decorative capital A. At the back: a cast type with its jet still attached, and a cast type dressed to form the finished sort at type height.

van den Keere, and Antoine Augereau are missing. But as well as the more famous names of Gutenberg, Granjon, and Bodoni, I have been able to include some lesser-known designers like Erhard Ratdolt, Simon de Colines, Johann Fleischman, and Alexander Phemister.

Four elements
Like the format of *Historical Scripts*, each spread has four elements – an illustration of a whole page from the selected book, an enlarged detail of the type, a small actual size sample, and a brief descriptive commentary.

An enormous amount of effort has been expended in order to find authentic, early examples of the historical types and, as far as possible, to show them used in 'normal' books. This is, after all, the way the types were intended to be used. Some types have proved rather elusive so, occasionally, I have had to resort to showing examples from type specimen books in order to be sure that the types illustrated are genuine. Finding authentic early examples of even the famous types of Garamont is not that easy, and many mistakes have been made in the past. The roman types of Jean Jannon bought by the Imprimerie royale in 1641 are almost impossible to find in actual use. The researches of James Mosley (see his *Typefoundry* blog, 3 February 2012), have shown that they were never used by the Imprimerie royale during the 17th century, despite the claims of Beatrice Warde and Henri-Jean Martin that they 'were used in splendid works during the early years of this institution'.

Every single image in this publication has been specially commissioned. The best pages for photography have been carefully selected from each book, not only to show an attractive page but also one which was cleanly printed. Often pages which have actually been *under*-inked show the type most clearly. Usually, the whole page with complete margins is shown, to set the type in its intended context. But a few of the book pages are so large and their types so small that, in order to facilitate better study of the type itself, in those cases an inset has been provided of the whole page and an extra section of the text shown at least at actual size.

The illustrations
Each enlarged detail of the type shows five lines of text, carefully chosen not only for its clarity of print but also to include as many different letters of the alphabet as possible. A missing letter from the enlargement is often included in the actual size detail.

These macro-enlargements are new high-resolution digital images captured with raking light. This reveals the impression of the metal type into the surface, the ink 'squeeze', and even the surface quality of the paper or vellum with a clarity and vividness which I believe has not been seen before. Each image has been scaled very accurately to a specified enlargement, one most appropriate for the particular type size and interlinear space of the example shown.

An actual size sample, conveniently positioned at the bottom of the second column of text, allows ready comparison with other types in the book.

The commentaries
As the primary aim is to provide a visual (and therefore more accessible) survey of historical type designs, space for commentary is limited. Nevertheless it is hoped that both student and teacher will find the notes helpful and detailed enough to enable further research. Background information has been provided where it has seemed to me to be relevant or interesting. My three-fold aim for the commentaries has been to be concise, accurately up-to-date, and worthwhile.

But having begun new research, it was not long before I realised that my brief college summaries were mere caricatures of the truth, and that I had totally overlooked some very important type designs. Even more significant, and disturbing, was the revelation that the traditional 'authorities' like Daniel Updike, Stanley Morison, Harry Carter, and others are now (perhaps inevitably) not always reliable. Much new research has been done since their laudable efforts, and so acquainting myself with the most recent and accurate 'palaeotypography' has been an essential part of my preparation for this book. Because of this, *Historical Types* has taken much longer to complete than I originally anticipated, but I have felt it right to spend the necessary extra effort and time to 'get it right', or at least as right as I can make it. After all, as I said in my Introduction to *Historical Scripts*, 'the student is not well-served by the nonchalant repetition of unsubstantiated ideas'! The motto of Aldus Manutius, *Festina lente* ('hurry up slowly'), has provided me with wise counsel throughout the more than three years of intense research.

THE NINETEENTH CENTURY
Surprisingly, one of the most difficult periods to survey has been the 19th century. Although it was an era of vigorous printing activity and prolific diversity of types, especially for display (some theatre and circus posters of the time incorporated a positive riot of ornate typefaces, all screaming for attention), book work remained more sober. Roman types were considered most appropriate, though even these varied hugely. Sometimes 'retro' traits were favoured, occasionally artificially 'antiqued' with toned paper stock and the revived use of long **s** (ſ), or even a return to medieval textura types, often with outrageously distorted forms *(Fig. 2)*. Fortunately, the latter were mostly reserved for 'ecclesiastical' use, perhaps under the (surely mistaken) impression that such types suggested a sense of Authority. It is amusing to note, even today, the mastheads of some national newspapers set in out-dated blackletter types, perhaps in the attempt to delude their readers into thinking that they purvey Truth.

Sans-serif types, capitals only, were first seen in the William Caslon IV Specimen of *c*. 1819. These were soon expanded into lowercase letters and were used in display situations everywhere. But when I discovered some sans-serif types, caps and lowercase, shown as *text sizes* (6pt–12pt) in *An Abridged Specimen of Fonts of Type* made at George Bruce's New York Type Foundry, dated November 1865 *(Fig 3)* it was a tantalising moment. Surely these sans-serifs were intended for far nobler things than business cards, classified ads, and railway timetables? Yet, despite searching high and low, I have found no 19th-century example of sans-serif type used for the text of journals or books.

GUTENBERG AND HIS METHODS

Gutenberg has been celebrated as the 'Inventor of the Millennium' in the popular poll organised by the BBC in January 2000 and rightfully so, for the invention of a fully integrated system of printing from movable type was a seminal development. It enabled the much wider sharing and preservation of information, all across Europe, and made possible the multiplication of books with identical texts. Rival claims to the invention have been raised in the past, perhaps sometimes due to nationalist pride or local legend, but the documentary and circumstantial evidence is now overwhelmingly in support of the long-held traditional view that Johann Gutenberg of Mainz was indeed the first to print a substantial work by means of movable type. Questions remain, however, regarding the specific details of his working methods.

Most recently, scholars Paul Needham and Blaise Agüera y Arcas, have drawn attention to the fact that Gutenberg's printed letters vary considerably, quite apart from the deliberate inclusion of extra sorts like ligatures and abbreviations. Their new observations, documented by remarkable photographs and digital images, also reveal minute variations within individual letters, which seem to suggest that they were not made by striking a matrix with a punch. Their research raises valid questions about how Gutenberg actually cast his type, but their guesses about the use of clay moulds or sand casting, for example, are neither very practical nor will they result in the details of letter variations which they themselves observed.

Other evidence

Many scholars of typography, especially those who have practical printing experience, are not yet prepared to give up the traditional view that Gutenberg produced at least some of his types by means of punch, matrix, and adjustable mould. It certainly seems likely, as emphasised by De Vinne as far back as 1878, that Gutenberg must have used some form of adjustable mould to cast his type.

And there is some documentary evidence for very early use of punches and matrices in the making of type. Melissa Conway (1999) has published and transcribed a 15th-century document concerning the activities of a printing press in a convent at Ripoli. This records that goldsmiths from Florence cut punches and made matrices for the Ripoli press during the 1470s. In addition, there is an account of a visit of Nicolas Jenson to Mainz in October 1458 (an earlier date, so even more significant). Jenson was sent by Charles VII of France to discover more about the 'people skilled in cutting punches'. Lotte Hellinga (2003) re-examines the evidence and argues that it should be taken seriously.

Much further research, both practical and observational,

Top: Fig. 2 *Victoria* textura type, *double-english* size (*c.* 28pt), from *An Abridged Specimen of Fonts of Type*, George Bruce, New York, November 1865. Chicago, The Newberry Library, Wing z 40583 .1245.

Bottom: Fig. 3 *Gothic No. 4*, sans-serif type in four sizes (*c.* 6pt, 8pt, 10pt, and 12pt), from *An Abridged Specimen of Fonts of Type*, George Bruce, New York, November 1865. Chicago, The Newberry Library, Wing z 40583 .1245, page 42.

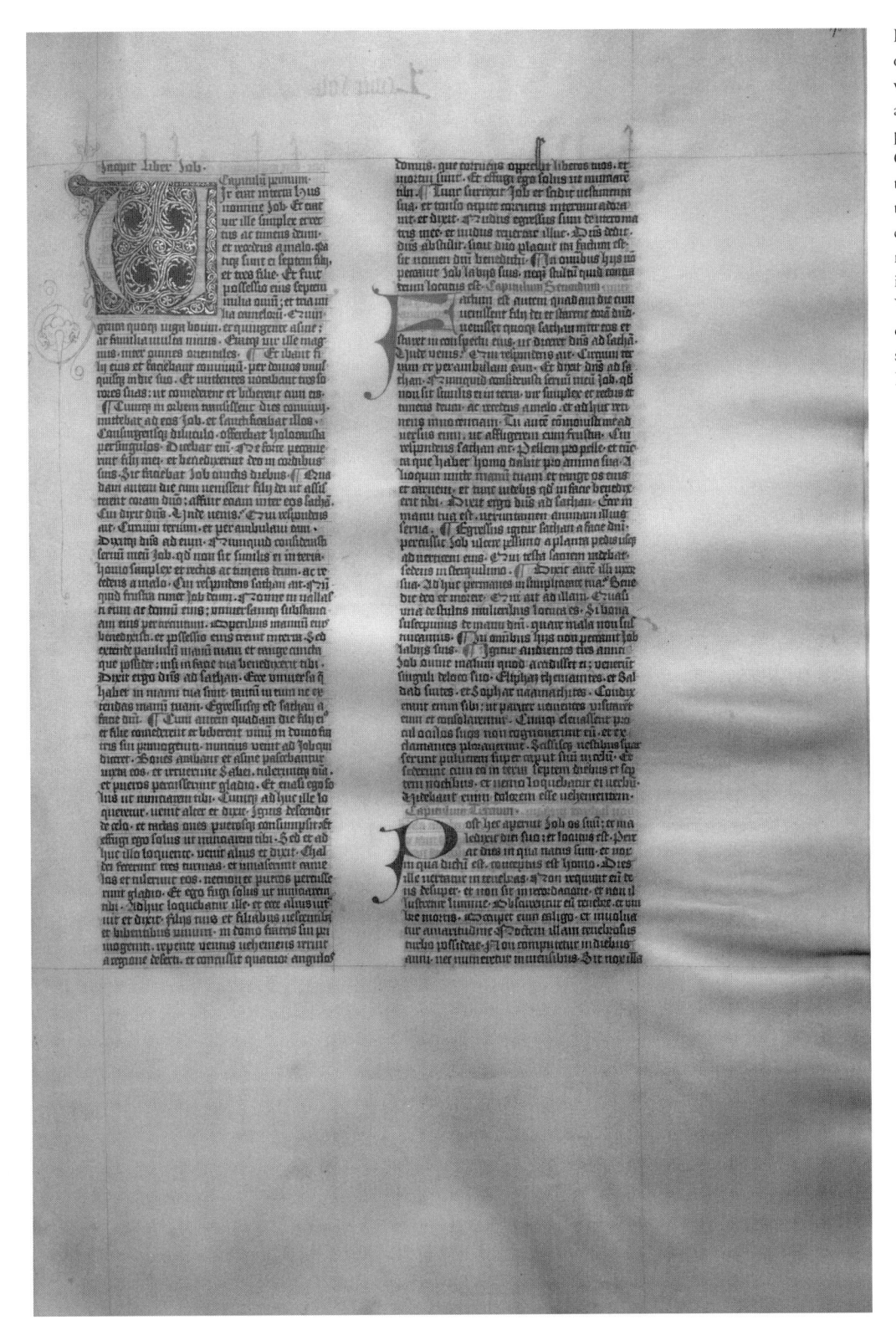

Fig. 4 The so-called 'Giant Bible of Mainz' (1452–1453), a handwritten manuscript produced about the same time as the printed 42-line Bible of Gutenberg (see *A2*). Note the similarities between them – the *mise-en-page*, double columns, textura letterforms, running heads, and large initials added by a rubricator. Washington DC, Library of Congress, Ms 8, folio 176R, showing the beginning of the Book of Job.

will be needed before the puzzle of Gutenberg's methods can be fully resolved. Meanwhile, we can still stand in awe at the remarkable ingenuity which resulted in those early types, and the extraordinary high level of printing he achieved.

CALLIGRAPHY AND THE FIRST TYPES

The earliest printed documents closely imitated the form of contemporary manuscripts. They had the same codex format with its sewn gatherings, the same *mise-en-page*, and the same letterform style. Compare the appearance and script of the 'Giant Bible of Mainz', which is a manuscript book *(Fig. 4)*, with Gutenberg's printed 42-line Bible *(A2)*. These were both produced in the same region, at about the same time, and the similarities are manifest. For one thing, the 42-line Bible follows scribal practice by incorporating a multitude of abbreviations, ligatures, and suspensions, far more

Fig. 5 Apocalysis Sancti Johannis, considered to be the earliest-known European blockbook. It was produced in Germany and dates from *c.* 1451. The whole of the text and the line illustrations were cut into the woodblock, in reverse, and printed on one side of each of the 48 leaves of this book. The lively illustrations were then delicately hand-coloured. Manchester, The John Rylands Library, JRL 3103, folio 44r, the 'Heavenly Jerusalem'.

than the basic 50 or so 'glyphs' needed for Latin text with caps and lowercase. Like many contemporary illuminated manuscripts Gutenberg's printed Bible was sold as loose gatherings, with spaces left for an illuminator to decorate, and for a rubricator to complete the coloured initial caps and running heads, before it was bound. Indeed, for the guidance of the scribe, he printed an eight-page supplement listing all the required headings.

The first printers, and their customers, were fully conscious of the symbiotic relationship between their printed books and the manuscripts they were replacing. The Mainz Psalter of 1457 (see *A3*) has a colophon which not only acknowledges that it has all the characteristics of a handwritten manuscript, but also emphasises that it was 'given this form artificially by means of a contrivance for printing and inscribing without any use of a pen'.

PRINTING BEFORE GUTENBERG

Of course, the technique of printing was not invented by Gutenberg. Books printed from woodblocks were made long before the 15th century. To produce these the design of the whole page, both illustrations and text, would be cut into a flat block of wood (in reverse). This would then be inked, and the image transferred to the paper by burnishing the back of the sheet. Until recently, the *Diamond Sutra* has been considered the earliest block book with text; it was printed *c.* 868. But now even earlier examples, from Korea, have been dated to the mid-8th century. The complex nature of oriental scripts is not conducive to the process of movable type, so printing by means of woodblocks like these continued for many centuries in the Far East. However, actual movable types, probably made from ceramic tiles, have been credited to Bí Sheng in China from early in the 11th century. And types cast in bronze were used to print documents in Korea more than 70 years before the experiments of Gutenberg.

Printing books with woodcuts developed surprisingly late in Europe. The earliest-known European book to be printed from woodcuts, the delightfully hand-coloured Apocalypse of John *(Fig. 5)*, has the text cut into the block just like its illustrations. It is now considered to date from *c.* 1451 – just prior to Gutenberg's novel use of type.

THE POINT SYSTEM

The accurate specification of the tiny increments of type sizes, by means of a universal point system, is a convenient one. Of course, the first printers cast their own type 'in house', so in fact there was little need at that time for similar type sizes between one printer and another. However, when typefounding became established as an independent activity, late in the 15th and early 16th centuries, more consistency in the various sizes of type became necessary. Towards the end of the 16th century, founders began to apply names to commonly used sizes of type. The specimens of Christophe Plantin and the Le Bé foundry, for example, gave names such as *brevier*, *canon*, and *great primer* (probably reflecting an ecclesiastical origin for the use of those particular sizes). Nevertheless inconsistencies in naming and sizing continued through most of the 17th and 18th centuries, especially from region to region. Complaints about this situation were aired by both Joseph Moxon, *Mechanick Exercises* (1683) and John Smith, *The Printer's Grammar* (1755).

Fournier & Truchet

In his *Modéles des Caractères* of 1742, Pierre-Simon Fournier included a standardised table of type measurements, later claiming, in his *Manuel Typographique* published in 1764, that he was the first to rationalise the existing confusion. But, much earlier, the Bignon Commission, which had been set up in 1693 to produce the new *romains du roi* for the Imprimerie royale, had also worked on a scheme for standardising the relationship between one size of type and another. Sébastien Truchet, a member of that Commission, drafted several versions of a scale of proportions to be followed for the 20 sizes to be cut for the *romains du roi*. Basing his scheme on the legal standard of the *pied-de-roi* (*c.* 32.5 cms), he divided the *pied* into 12 *pouce*, the *pouce* into 12 *lignes*, and then sub-divided each *ligne* into 12 *lignes seconde* (a unit measuring 0.188 mm). Instead of naming the incremental sizes of type he gave them a simple number (1st being the smallest and 16th the largest), with some half sizes in between. Not all the sizes in the scheme were actually cut. Philippe Grandjean was responsible for cutting 13 sizes of the *romains du roi*, beginning with the Alphabets *Neuvième* (*c.*16pt) and *Dixième* (*c.* 20pt), both used for the sumptuous book, *Médailles de Louis le Grand* printed in 1702 (see *E1*).

The Truchet system seems to have been followed throughout the 18th century for all sizes of the *romains du roi* and, of course, this pre-dated Fournier's 'invention' by nearly 50 years. It is hard to believe that Fournier was completely unaware of the Commission's scheme.

Didot

François-Ambroise Didot established his foundry about 1783. It was at this time that he published his own system for type measurement. Fournier's earlier 'Table of proportions' seems to have been just the rationalisation of existing foundry practice and had no independent standard of measurement. He simply printed an arbitrary typescale as a guide for others to follow. Didot, however, tied his point system to the old legal standard of the *pied-de-roi* (previously used by Sébastien Truchet for the Bignon Commission), but his basic unit of the point was twice the size of Truchet's *ligne seconde*.

It took a long time for the Didot point to gain general acceptance, but by 1840s it was adopted as the official standard in France, and then Germany in 1879. Later it was also adopted by Scandinavia, Russia, Spain, Italy, South America, and the Near East. The Anglo-American point was the accepted measurement in areas of English-speaking influence (despite the irrationality of 72 points equalling 0.9936 of an inch). Now the *digital* Anglo-American point has been rounded up to exactly 72pts to the inch (12pts to the pica, 6 picas to the inch).

The meticulous researches of James Mosley have clarified and disentangled the complex and often confusing accounts of the historical standardisation of the measurement of type (see, for example, his *Typefoundry* blog, 30 April 2008).

ORTHOGRAPHY

In *Historical Types* I have adopted the manner of referring to type styles and calligraphic hands without an initial capital – 'roman', 'italic', 'uncial' etc. Of course this leads to a certain awkwardness when applied to 'greek' and 'hebrew' types. But whichever usage is applied, some awkwardness occurs. With 'sans-serif' I have played safe, tempting though it is to render it as 'sanserif'.

And, after a lifetime of doing otherwise, I have now deferred to Hendrik Vervliet and others, regarding the spelling of 'Claude Garamont' for the famous 16th-century French punchcutter; retaining 'Garamond' to identify the modern typefaces named after him (only a couple of which are actually derived from his work). The historical evidence is mixed and far from conclusive (see Mosley, *Typefoundry* blog, 1 April 2011, for an extensive discussion of the question), but in the imprints of books he himself published with Jean Barbé in 1545, he signed himself 'Claude Garamont'. So maybe that is enough. The real irony is that in French, at least, they both sound exactly the same.

Stan Knight
Bonners Ferry, Idaho
on the Feast of Pentecost, 2012

Uniuersis Cristifidelibus p[rese]ntes l[itte]ras inspecturis **Paulinus** Chappe Co[n]siliari[us] A[m]ba[s]iator & p[ro]curator generalis Sereni[ssi]mi Regis Cypri in hac parte Salut[em] in d[omi]no Cu[m] Sanctissim[us] i[n] x[pi]o p[ate]r & d[omi]n[u]s n[oste]r d[omi]n[u]s Nicolaus diui[n]a p[ro]uide[n]tia p[a]p[a] quint[us] Afflicti[on]i Regni Cypri m[isericor]dit[er] co[m]patiens co[n]tra p[er]fidiss[im]o[s] crucis xpi hostes Theucros & Saracenos gratis co[n]cessit om[n]ib[us] xpifidelib[us] vbilibet [con]stitutis ipos p a[s]p[er]sio[n]e sanguis d[omi]ni n[ost]ri ih[es]u xpi pie exhortado qui infra trieniu[m] a prima die Maij Anni d[omi]ni M°ccccliij i[n]cipie[n]du[m] p[ro] defe[n]sio[n]e catho[]lice fidei & regni p[re]d[i]c[t]i de facultatibus suis magis uel min[us] put ipor[um] videbitur [con]scie[n]tijs p[ro]cu[ra]torib[us] uel nu[n]cijs substitutis pie eroga[]uerint ut Confessores ydoneos seculares uel regulares p ipos elige[n]di [con]fessionib[us] eor[um] auditis. p co[m]missis etia[m] sedi ap[osto]lice reseruatis excessib[us] criminib[us] atq[ue] delictis q[ua]ntu[m]cu[m]q[ue] grauib[us] p vna vice tantu[m] debita[m] absolutione[m] impe[n]dere & penite[n]tia[m] salutarem iniu[n]gere Reno[]ua[n]do suis hu[mili]t[er] petierit ipos a quibuscu[m]q[ue] ex[com]municationu[m] suspensionu[m] & interdicti alijs[que] sente[n]cijs ce[n]suris & penis ecclesiasticis a iure uel ab ho[m]i[n]e p[ro]mulgatis quib[us] for[s]an i[n]nodati exsti[te]rint absoluere. Iniu[n]cta p modo culpe p[e]nite[n]tia salutari uel alijs q[ue] de iure fuerit iniu[n]ge[n]da ac eis vere penite[n]tib[us] [con]fessis uel si fors[a]n propter amissione[m] loq[ue]le [con]fiteri no[n] poterit signa [con]triconis ostede[n]do plenissima o[mn]iu[m] p[ec]co[rum] suor[um] de quib[us] ore [con]fessi & corde [con]triti fuerint Indulgentia ac plenaria remissione[m] semel in vita & semel in mortis articulo ipis au[c]te ap[osto]lica [con]cedere valeat. Satisfactione p eos facta si supuixerint aut p eor[um] heredes si tu[n]c tra[n]sierit Sic tame[m] [quod] post indultu[m] aplicu[m] p vnu[m] annu[m] singulis sextis ferijs uel q[uo]uis alia die ieiune[n]t. legitti[m]o i[m]pedime[n]to ecclesie p[re]cepto regulari obseruantia p[e]nia iniu[n]cta voto uel alias no[n] obstan[]. Et si ip[s]is impediti[s] in dicto a[n]no uel eius parte. anno sequeti uel alias quam primu[m] poterint ieiunabu[n]t Et si in aliquo anno, uel eor[um] parte dict[um] ieiuniu[m] co[m]mode adimplere nequiuerit Confessor ad id electus in alia [com]mutare poterit caritatis opa q[uod] ipsi facere etia[m] tenentur D[um]modo ti[ame]n [con]fidentia remissionis huiusmodi q[uod] absit peccare no[n] p[re]sumat Alioqui dicta [con]cessio quo ad plenaria[m] remissione[m] in mortis articulo et remissio quo ad p[ec]ca ex [con]fidentia ut p[re]mittit[ur] co[m]missa nullius sint roboris uel mo[m]enti Et quia deuoti ~~~~~~~~~~ iuxta dictum indultu[m] de facultatibus suis pie eroga[ue]r[unt] merito huiusmodi indulgentijs gaudere debet. In veritatis testimoniu[m] sigillu[m] ad hoc ordinatu[m] p[rese]ntib[us] l[itte]ris testimonialib[us] est appe[n]sum Datu[m] Colo[n] Anno d[omi]ni M°cccclij die vero ~~~~ mensis ~~~~

forma plenissime absolutionis et remissionis in vita

Misereatur tui &c. D[omi]n[u]s noster Ihesus xpus p sua[m] sanctissima[m] et pijssima[m] m[isericord]ia[m] te absoluat Et au[c]te ipi[us] beator[um]q[ue] petri & pauli ap[osto]lor[um] eius ac au[c]te ap[osto]lica michi [com]missa & tibi [con]cessa Ego te absoluo ab omib[us] p[ecca]tis tuis [con]tritis [con]fessis & oblitis Etia[m] ab omib[us] casib[us] excessib[us] criminib[us] atq[ue] delictis quantu[m]cu[m]q[ue] grauib[us] sedi ap[osto]lice reseruatis Reno[]ua[n]do a quibuscu[m]q[ue] ex[com]municationu[m] suspensionu[m] & interdicti Alijs[que] sente[n]cijs ce[n]suris & penis ecclesiasticis a iure uel ab ho[m]i[n]e p[ro]mulgatis si quas incurristi dando tibi plenissima[m] oim p[ec]cor[um] tuor[um] indulgentia[m] & remissione[m] Inq[uan]tu[m] claues sancte matris ecc[les]ie in hac parte se extendu[n]t. In no[m]i[n]e patris & filij & spiritus sancti Amen.

forma plenarie remissionis in mortis articulo

Misereatur tui &c. D[omi]n[u]s noster ut supra Ego te absoluo ab omib[us] p[ec]c[a]tis tuis [con]tritis [con]fessis & oblitis restituendo te vnitati fideliu[m] & sacramentis ecclesie Remittendo tibi penas purgatorij quas propter culpas & offensas incurristi dando tibi plenaria[m] oim p[ec]cor[um] tuor[um] remissione[m]. Inq[uan]tu[m] claues sancte matris ecc[les]ie in hac parte se extendu[n]t. In no[m]i[n]e patris & filij & spiritus sancti Amen.

Medieval Types   *Johann Gutenberg A1*

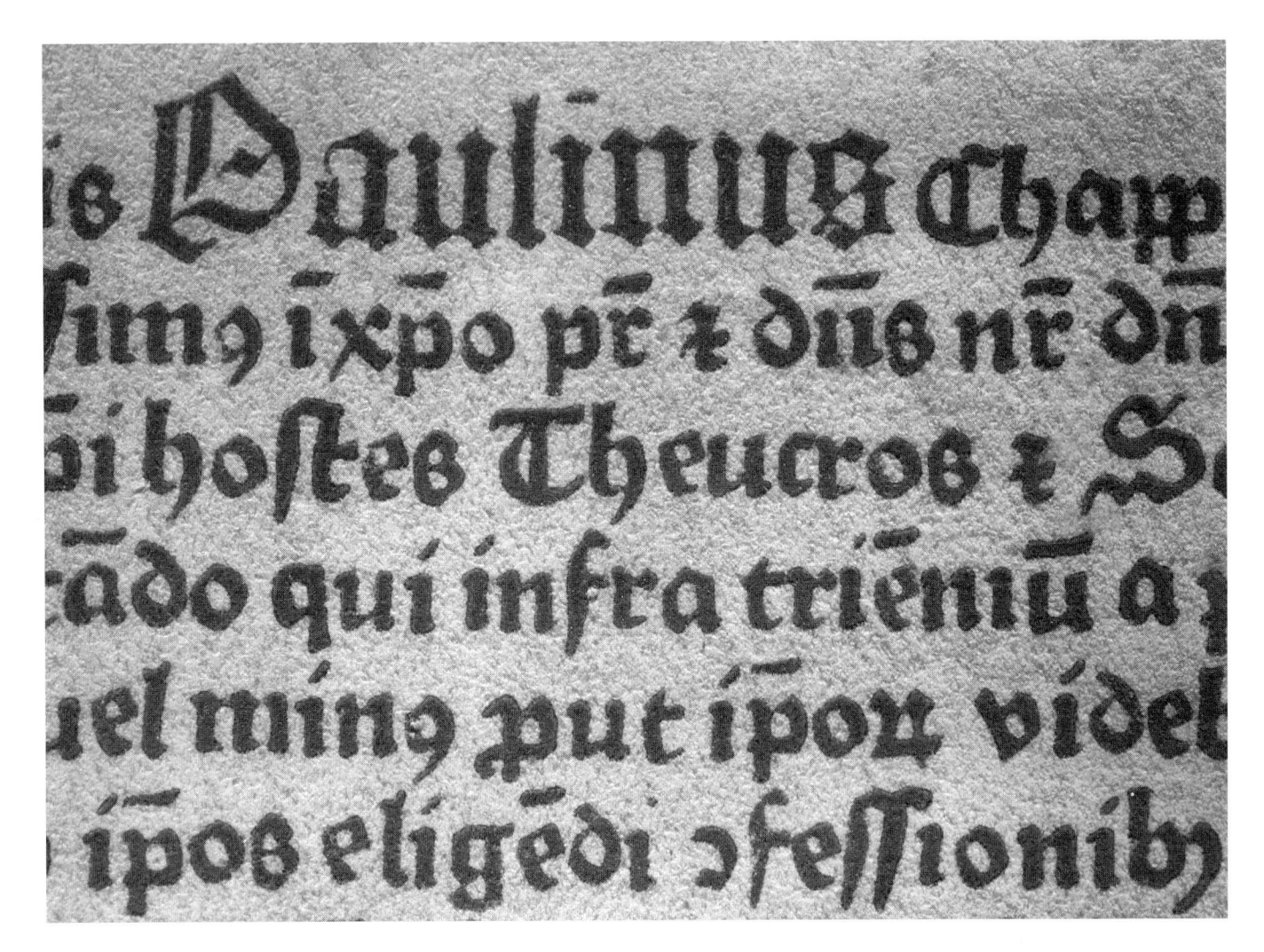

Manchester, The John Rylands Library, JRL 17250.1. *Certificate of Indulgence*. Printed in Mainz, Germany in 1454 by Johann Gutenberg (*c.* 1400–1468).

The size of the vellum sheet is 7⅞" x 11" (201 x 279 mm). The text measure is 9" wide (228 mm). The enlargement is shown at four and a half times actual size.

While Gutenberg's 42-line Bible is, without question, his most important printed work, it seems inconceivable that he would *begin* his ground-breaking endeavours with such a mammoth undertaking. He must have experimented first with other, much less ambitious, pieces of printing.

This Letter of Indulgence was certainly printed before the Bible was completed, yet it is a sophisticated piece of printing. It uses two different sizes of type, and wood- or metal-engraved initial letters inserted into the forme with the type.

By 1454 Gutenberg's work in developing a means of printing by type must have become known beyond Mainz. He was commissioned to make this Indulgence, and his press proved to be the perfect method of reproducing a large quantity of identical documents. Spaces were left in the printed text (lines 18 and 20) for the name of the donor and date to be inserted by hand at the time of purchase.

More than thirty copies of this Gutenberg Indulgence are known, and all were purchased between 22 October 1454 and 30 April 1455. Among them, variant editions of the Indulgence have been noted, each with slightly different wording, layout, and types. This one in the John Rylands Library is unique, and has the earlier printed date of 1454 ('Mccccliiii', line 20). It was issued to a certain Georgius de Arnisbergh of Cologne and his wife Frederica on 27 February 1455 (note the written amendment to the printed year).

The textura display type is the same as that used for the text of the 42-line Bible (see *A2*). The tiny gothic type is unusual; note its round **a** and **d**, 'uncial' **h**, cursive **f**, and long **s** (ſ). It has an x-height of just 2 mm. The letters are actually not well-aligned (in his Bible printing this was improved), and some over-inking and ink squeeze is apparent.

Many extra sorts are employed, all typical of current scribal practice. There are numerous ligatures, including ct, ff, pp, ſſ, ſl, ft, and an unusual **ij** (line 4); lots of abbreviations (indicated by a horizontal line over the word); and some suspensions (such as ♃, ϡ) and contractions (like reversed Ↄ), representing missing syllables (the last word in the enlargement above, for example, is 'confessionibus'). Note alternate forms of **r** and **s**, and the rare **y** (lines 2 and 6, see detail below). The ⁊ character is a medieval form of ampersand.

15

abisset puer surrexit dauid de loco qui
vergebat ad austrū: et cadens pronus
ī terrā. adorauit tercio. Et osculātes se
alterutrū. fleuerunt pariter. dauid autē
āpli9. Dixit ergo yonathas ad dauid.
Uade in pace. Quecūq; iurauimus
ambo in nomine domini. dicentes:
domin9 sit inter me et te. et inter semen
tuum z semen meum. usq; in sempiter-
num. Et surrexit dauid et abijt: sed et
yonathas ingressus e ciuitate. XXI
V̄enit autē dauid in nobe. ad achimelech sacerdotē. Et obstupuit
achimelech. eo quod uenisset dauid. z
dixit ei. Quare tu solus: et nullus est
tecum? Et ait dauid ad achimelech sa-
cerdotem. Rex precepit michi sermonem.
et dixit. Nemo sciat rem propter quā
missus es a me: z cuiusmodi precepta
tibi dederi. Nā et pueris meis cōdixi. ī

hic ad manū hastam aut gladiū da
michi: quia gladiū meū z arma mea
non tuli mecum. Sermo enim regis
vrgebat. Et dixit sacerdos. Ecce hic
gladi9 goliath philistei. quē percussisti
in valle therebinti. est inuolut9 pallio
post ephot. Si istum vis tollere. tolle.
Neq; eni hic est alius absq; eo. Et ait
dauid. Nō est huic alter similis. Da
michi eū. Surrexit itaq; dauid. z fugit
ī die illa a facie saul: z venit ad achis
regem geth. Dixerūtq; sui achis: cum
uidissent dauid. Nūquid non iste est
dauid rex terre? Nōne huic cātabant
per choros dicētes: percussit saul mille.
z dauid decem milia? Posuit autem
dauid sermones istos in corde suo: z
extimuit valde a facie achis regis geth.
Et mutauit os suū corā achis. et col-
labebatr̄ inter manus eo℞: et impinge-
bat in hostia porte: defluebātq; saliue
eius in barbā. Et ait achis ad seruos
suos. Vidistis hominem insanum:
q̄re adduxistis eū ad me? An desint
nobis furiosi: qa introduxistis istum
ut fureret me p̄sente? Dimittite illum
hinc: ne ingrediatr̄ domū meā. XXII
A̅bijt ergo dauid inde: et fugit in
speluncā odollam. Quod cum
audissent fr̄es ei9 et omnis dom9 pris
eius: descēderūt ad eū illuc. Et cōuene-
runt ad eū omnes qui erāt in angustia
cōstituti. et oppssi ere alieno et amaro
aio: et scūs est eo℞ princeps. Fuerūtq;
cū eo q̄si quadringēti viri. Et pfectus
est dauid inde in masphat. q̄ est moab.

Medieval Types *Johann Gutenberg A2*

Manchester, The John Rylands Library, JRL 3069. *The 42-line Bible*. Printed in Mainz, Germany in 1455.

The page size is 15⅝" x 11" (397 x 281 mm). The column measure is 3½" (90 mm). The book is in two volumes with }a total of 643 folios. The whole-page reproduction is taken from volume I, folio 141V, the enlargement (three and a half times actual size) from volume I, folio 260R.

This is the famous 42-line Bible of Johann Gutenberg, which as far as we know, is the first substantial book ever printed by moveable type in Europe. Some 48 copies and extensive fragments survive, a quarter of them printed on vellum. A copy in the Bibliothèque nationale in Paris has a handwritten colophon stating that the rubricator finished his work on St Bartholomew's Day (24 August) in 1456. This clearly implies that some copies of this Gutenberg Bible must have been completed by the end of 1455.

The general appearance of the 42-line Bible was obviously copied from contemporary manuscripts. The page layout, the letterforms, the frequent use of abbreviations and ligatures, and the use of vellum (excellent to write on, but difficult to print on), all followed current scribal practice.

Some copies of the 42-line Bible contain certain pages which only have 40 lines of text. It seems that Gutenberg began with just 40 lines, but soon realised that he needed to include more in order to reduce the total number of pages. The 40-line pages occur in four different places in the Bible, strongly suggesting that he was actually using four separate presses and dividing the work between them. A few surviving copies have those pages reset with the full 42 lines per page. Ambitiously, some of those 40-line pages also have the headings printed in red. As this entailed a second impression for each page, this scheme was soon abandoned, so spaces were left for a scribe to complete the text by hand, in colour.

The type of the 42-line Bible copies the large textura script used at that time for Missals and other liturgical manuscripts (see *Introduction, Fig. 4*). It includes 300 different letterform glyphs (a multitude of abbreviations, ligatures and shorthand characters), far more than the basic 50 or so needed for Latin text with capitals and lowercase. In the enlargement, for example, note the ligatures **do, ff, ft**, even **ve**; others may be found on the page opposite.

Considering that this was the first major book ever printed, the result is astonishing. Gutenberg selected fine vellum and paper. He developed an excellent ink for both, and his typesetting and presswork gave a crisp, clear impression. It is probable that Peter Schoeffer assisted him during this period, and given the superior quality of the Psalter printed just two years later (see *A3)*, the finer aspects of even the 42-line Bible could well be attributed to Schoeffer.

tuis nati sunt tibi filij: constitues eos principes
sup omnem terram. Memor ero nois tui:
in omni generacōe et generacōe. Propterea
ppli confitebuntur tibi in eternum: et in seclm secli.

Eructauit cor meum verbum bonum. Adiutor. Eya aue
Deus noster refugium et vir= Psalmus
tus: adiutor in tribulationibz que
inuenerunt nos nimis. Propterea non time=
bimus dum turbabitur terra: et transferentur montes
in cor maris. Sonuerunt et turbate sunt
aque eorum: conturbati sunt montes in fortitudine
eius. Fluminis impetus letificat ciuitatem dei:
sanctificauit tabernaclm suum altissimus. Deus
in medio eius non commouebitur: adiuuabit eam
deus mane diluculo. Conturbate sunt gentes et in=
clinata sunt regna: dedit vocem suam mota e tra.
Dominus virtutum nobiscum: susceptor noster deus ia=
cob. Venite et videte opera domini que posuit prodigia
sup tram: auferens bella usque ad finem tre. Arcum

Medieval Types   *Johann Fust & Peter Schoeffer A3*

Manchester, The John Rylands Library, JRL 9784. *The Mainz Psalter.* Printed in Mainz, Germany in 1457.

The page size is 15¼" x 9⅛" (385 x 230 mm). (This copy has been brutally cropped in rebinding.) The text measure is 7⅞" (200 mm). The book has 286 pages. The whole-page reproduction is taken from page 108, the enlargement (one and three quarter times actual size) from page 39.

Johann Fust, a wealthy banker, had been in partnership with Gutenberg, lending him money for his printing endeavour. A lawsuit in November 1455 reveals that Gutenberg was unable to repay his debt and so all his printing equipment passed to Fust and his son-in-law Peter Schoeffer. A colophon in this Psalter records the completion of the work on 14 August 1457 and also names Fust and Schoeffer as the printers and publishers. Peter Schoeffer was a calligrapher, born in Gernsheim, who worked for a while in Paris before moving to Mainz. There, providentially, he met Gutenberg and worked with him, most likely (in view of his experience with letterforms) designing and cutting types.

Ten copies of this 1457 Psalter survive, plus some fragments, all of them printed on vellum. Another Psalter was printed by Fust and Schoeffer just two years later, using the same type, and 13 copies of that edition survive. They deliberately followed the style of contemporary manuscripts for their books. A colophon in both Mainz Psalters states that although it has all the characteristics of a handwritten manuscript, it has been 'given the form artificially by means of a contrivance for printing and inscribing without the use of the pen'. It is an extremely elaborate production, printed in three colours, set in two sizes of text type, with many printed versal-style initials. The intricately decorated initials used at the beginning of each Psalm, such as the two-line **D** opposite and the four-line **D** (see *Historical Types* cover), were made up of several tightly 'nesting' metal engravings which had to be lifted out of the forme, separately inked, and replaced for each printing – obviously, a difficult and extremely time-consuming operation.

The type is a huge textura gothic. (See *Historical Scripts D3* and *D5* for very similar handwritten forms.) As with Gutenberg's founts (in *A1* and *A2*), the type for this Psalter includes numerous extra sorts. In the enlargement above note the ligatures **ct**, **de**, and **ho**; alternate forms of **r**, **s**, and **v**; the shorthand symbols of reversed ꝯ (for 'con') and ampersand ⁊ (for 'et'); and abbreviations indicated with a horizontal line. See numerous other examples opposite.

19

I se wel that lernyd men in love
Conne moche good be goddis dignite
The Parson hym answerde benedicite
What eylith the man so sinfully to swere
Oure oste answerde Jankyn be ye there
I smelle a lollere in the wynd quod he
Now good men quod our host herkneth me
Abidith for goddis digne passioun
For we shul haue now a predicacion
This lollare wol preche vs here sum what
Nay be my fader soule that shal he nat
Sayde the squyer he shal not here preche
He shal no gospel glose here ne teche
We leue alle in the grete god quod he
He wolde sowe sum difficulte
Or speynh cokyl in our clene corn
And therfore ofte I warne the beforn
My ioly body shal a tale telle
And I shal clynke yow so mery a belle
That it shal wakyn al this company
But it shal not be of philosophy
Ne of phisik ne termes queynte of lawe
There is but litil latin in my mawe

¶ Here begynneth the Squyers tale.
At Sarrey in the londe of Tartarye
There dwellid a kyng þ warrid on russy
Thorow whiche ther dyde many a doughty man
This nobyl kyng was clepid Cambuscan
Whiche in his tyme was of so greet renoun

Medieval Types   *William Caxton* A4

Manchester, The John Rylands Library, JRL 11567. Geoffrey Chaucer, *The Canterbury Tales*. Printed in Westminster, England in 1476 or early 1477 by William Caxton.

The page size is 9⅝" x 6⅞" (244 x 175 mm). The overall text measure is 5" (127 mm). The book has 374 folios. The whole-page reproduction is taken from folio 97v, the enlargement (three and a half times actual size) from folio 161v.

William Caxton was born in the Weald of Kent in the early 1420s. He was apprenticed in 1438 to Robert Lange, an eminent Mercer (later to become Lord Mayor of London). Caxton settled in Bruges in Belgium about 1443 and worked there for nearly 30 years, becoming a prominent diplomat. From 1471 he lived in Cologne where he learned about the craft of printing, most probably from Ulrich Zell of Mainz. During that time Caxton had his first three books printed.

He moved to Ghent in 1472 and set up his own press, publishing a further seven books, including the very first in the English language, the *Recuyell of the histories of Troy*. This, he tells us in his Preface, he translated from the French himself, at the behest of his patron, Margaret, Duchess of Burgundy. After a short while in Bruges Caxton finally returned to London in 1476 and he established the first printing press in England in the precincts of Westminster Abbey.

Caxton was not a printer in the modern sense. He certainly did not cut his own type, and it is unlikely that he involved himself in the actual printing process. Yet before he died in 1492 he had published over 100 titles, the majority in English. At a time when books printed in the vernacular were extremely rare in Europe (the use of Latin was normal), Caxton's determination to publish texts in English not only created a new class of reader, but it also stimulated the use of English as an appropriate language for the printed word.

The Canterbury Tales was the first major book printed in England. Paper stock analysis has now shown that it was completed before Caxton's *Dictes or Sayengis of the Philosophhres* (one copy of the latter is dated 18 November 1477).

The gothic bâtarde type used in *The Canterbury Tales* was made for Caxton by the gifted Flemish punchcutter, Johan Veldener. It is similar to a script used in the Bruges workshop of Colard Mansion. See *Historical Scripts (D6)* for a bâtarde written within 20 years of Caxton's printed book. Its angular style, unusual forms, and numerous ligatures make it rather difficult for the modern reader to decipher. In the enlargement above note the joined **be, co, da, de, ha, he, pr, re,** and **ti**. Note also the heavily-looped ascenders; 'cursive' **f** and **ſ**; the alternate forms for **r** and **s**; the tall **w**; and the flourish added to terminal **d**, and **n**. The capital forms are very ornate, but they closely follow the manuscript exemplar. The large handwritten versal **A**, inserted by a rubricator, partially covers a small, printed, guide letter.

21

per circuli circũferentiam duobus punctis signatis. li/
neam rectam ductam ab altero ad alterum. circulum seca
re necesse est.

Sit vt in circũferentia circuli.a.b.cuius centruʒ sit.c.signata sint
duo puncta que sunt.a.ʒ.b.dico q̃ linea recta coniũgens vnũ cum
bit circulum. Alioquin cadet extra circulum: sitqʒ.a.e.b.linea recta
producã lineas.c.a.ʒ.c.b.erũtqʒ per.5.primi: angulus.c.a.b.ʒ.c.
otraham itẽ lineã.c.e.que secet circãferentiam in puncto.d. eritqʒ
ngulus.a.e.c.maior angulo.c.b.e.quare maior angulo.c.a.c. qua
em latus.a.c.maius latere.c.e.ʒ quia.c.d.est equalis.c.a.erit.c.d
s toto quod est impossibile: quia ergo linea coniungens duo pũcta
bit extra circulum secabit ipsum quod est propositum.

Propositio .3.

lineam intra circulum preter centrum collocatam. alia
equa secet.orthogonaliter sup eam
thogonaliter steterit. eam p equa/

catã intra circulum.a.b.cuius centrum sit
a: dico q̃ diuidit eam orthogonaliter.ʒ e
onaliter diuidit eam per equalia. producã
at eã per eq̃lia: erũt ergo duo latera.c.d.
teribus.c.d.ʒ.d.b.trianguli.c.d.b.ʒ ba/
us.d.vnius est equalis angulo.d. alterius
ndicularis super.a.b.q̃d est propositum.
aris super.a.b.ʒ ostendam q̃ ipsa diui/
positionẽ vterqʒ angulox qui sunt ad.d

Medieval Types   *Erhard Ratdolt A5*

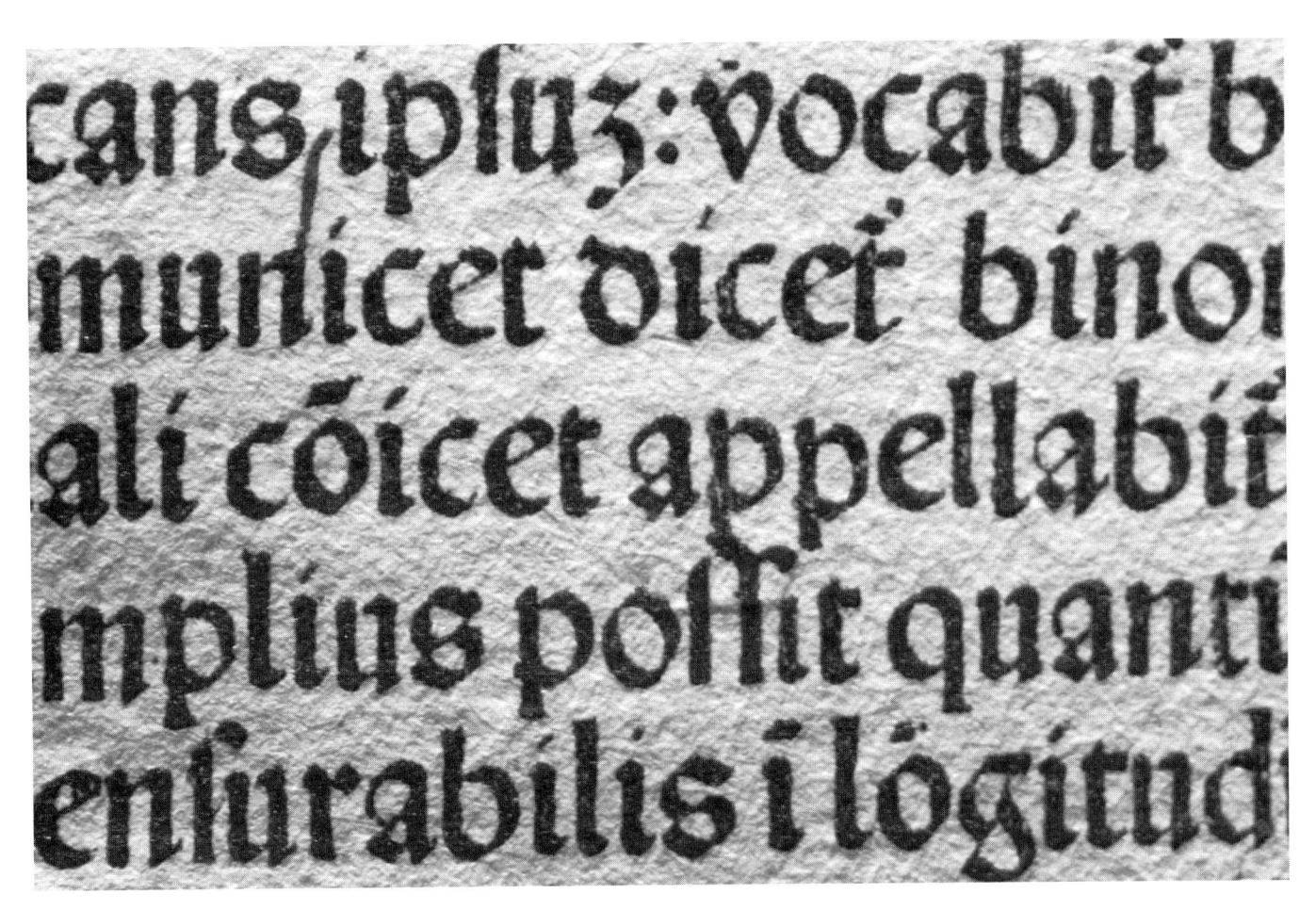

Chicago, The Newberry Library, INC. 4383. Euclides, *Elementia geometriae*. Printed in Venice, Italy in May 1482.

The page size is 11¾" x 8¼" (297 x 212 mm). The text measure is 4¾" (118 mm). The book has 138 folios. The whole-page reproduction is taken from folio 15v, the enlargement (four and a half times actual size) from folio 80r.

Erhard Ratdolt was a German printer, born in Augsburg in 1447, who moved to Venice in 1476. He must have known Nicolas Jenson there, and he is considered to have been the best printer in Venice after Jenson.

Ratdolt was an innovator. He was the earliest printer to include a separate title page in his books (in his *Kalendarius* of 1476). He used woodcuts for elaborate printed initials to ornament his pages, as can be seen in this book. In 1486, when he had returned to Augsburg, he printed a fine specimen sheet of his types which, as far as we know, was the very first typeface specimen ever produced. It was extensive, containing ten sizes of rotunda types, three of roman, one greek face, and a sample decorated initial.

The *Elementia geometricae* could well be a result of Ratdolt's collaboration with Johann Müller (Regiomontanus), a famous astronomer and mathematician, whom Ratdolt met in Nuremberg just before he moved to Venice.

Ratdolt dedicated this work, dated 25 May 1482, to the Doge of Venice, Giovanni Moncenigo. In his dedication Ratdolt states that despite the proliferation of printed books in his day, there was a dearth of scientific works because no means had yet been devised to reproduce geometric diagrams in print. But Ratdolt had been able to accomplish what others could not, and there are 420 detailed geometric diagrams in this book. It has long been presumed that these diagrams were printed from exceptionally skilful wood engravings, but recent thorough research by Renzo Baldasso (2009) suggests that Ratdolt used 'type high' metal strips, bent to shape and mounted in metal or wooden supports. John Boardley, however, considers the possibility that they may have been printed from large metal castings (*Codex 01*, 2011).

The British Library copy of the Euclides is the actual book presented to the Doge. It is printed on vellum, and the dedication itself is printed in gold. Bettina Wagner (2009) believes that Ratdolt used gold leaf for this, somehow adapting the bookbinder's methods of gold tooling.

Although Ratdolt on other occasions used roman types, the text of this impressive book is printed gothic rotunda, a common manuscript hand in 15th-century Italy. See a fine example in *Historical Scripts (F1)*. Two different sizes of type are skilfully used to clarify this complex mathematical text.

Note the 'broken' form of **g**, the rounded **h**, and the ornate text capitals (all typical of the handwritten rotunda script). There are variant forms for **r** and **s**, but **v** is used consistently. While some shorthand symbols occur, especially in the smaller type, there are few ligatures or abbreviations used. Note particularly the early use of 'arabic' numerals.

23

militaris nisi unum habeat ducem atq; rectorem. Quod si in uno exerci[tu]
fuerint impatores quot legiones: quot cohortes: quot cunei: quot al[e]
mu nec influi poterit acies uno quoq; periculu recusante: nec regi fac[ile]
temperari: quod suis ppriis consiliis utant omnes quoq; diuersitates
noceat q psint. Sed i hoc rex nature imperio nisi unus fuerit ad que t[otius]
summe cura referatur uniuersa soluent & corruent. Dicere aute mult[orum]
arbitrio regi mundu: tale e quale si quis affirmet i uno corpore multa[s esse]
mentes: quoniam multa & uaria sunt ministeria membrox ut singulos [cor]
poris sensus singule metes regere credant. Item multi affectus quibu[s]
moueri solemus uel ad iram uel ad cupiditatem: uel ad letitia uel ad [metum]
uel ad miserationem ut in his omnibus totidem mentes putentur ope[rari]

ca. iiij. Et sub uno humili deo pfectulares plures esse no possent

Quod si quis pfecto dicat: ne ipam qdem que una e habere uid[etur]
[in uno c]orpore tantaru reru gubernatione mens una p[ossit]
[& uniuersis simul i]ntenta e: cur aliquis existimet mudum no pos[se ab]
[uno regi: a pluribus p]osse. Quod qa intelligunt isti assertores deox it[a eos]
[presse singulis rebus a]c ptibus dicunt ut tame unus sit rector eximiu[s]
[Iam ergo ceteri dii non erun]t sed satellites ac ministri quos ille unus maxi[mus]
[& potens omniu officiis] his prefecerit: & ipi eius imperio ac nutibus [seruiant]
[si uniuersa partes] no sunt: no igitur dii omnes sunt. Nec enim p[otest]
[hoc idem esse quod seruit] et quod dominat. Nam si deus est nomen sum[me]
[potestatis i corruptibilis] esse debet: pfectus impassibilis: nulli rei sbiec[tus]
[ergo dii non sunt quos] parere uni maximo deo necessitas cogit. Sed q[uare]

Italian Renaissance Types   *Sweynheym & Pannartz   B1*

Chicago, The Newberry Library, INC. 3288. Lactantius, *De divinis institutionibus*. Printed in Subiaco, Italy in 1465.

The page size is 12⅛" x 8" (308 x 204 mm). The text measure is 5⅛" (130 mm). The book has 182 folios. The whole-page reproduction is taken from folio 13v, the enlargement (four times actual size) from folio 75R.

Konrad Sweynheym and Arnold Pannartz founded the very first press in Italy in the Benedictine monastery of Santa Scholastica in Subiaco towards the end of 1464. They were both printers from Germany. Sweynheym had worked with Peter Schoeffer in Mainz, and Pannartz came from the city of Cologne. In the two years that they were at Subiaco they produced four books: a Donatus Latin Grammar, this Lactantius, a Cicero, *De oratore*, and a work by Augustine, *De civitate dei*.

These letterforms of Sweynheym and Pannartz were considered by Stanley Morison to be the earliest example of a 'roman' typeface. He emphasised their overall 'humanistic' style: long ascenders and descenders, straight-backed **d**, closed **g**, arrow-headed **t**, and double-bodied **a**. But all these features occur in earlier protogothic and gothic rotunda scripts (see *Historical Scripts*, D2 and F1). And because of its heavy letter strokes, lateral compression, 'square' character, and its exaggerated stress, this type may be better categorised as 'semi-gothic' or, as Ehrle and Liebaert described Petrarch's handwriting of 1370, 'fere-humanistica' *(almost humanist)!* This type was actually copied for use by the Ashendene Press in 1902, and they called it *Subiaco* (see H3 notes).

Sweynheym and Pannartz moved to Rome in the autumn of 1467 and the later type they used there resembled more our modern concept of roman letterforms, but even that cannot compare with the elegant and fully-developed roman type of 1470 by Nicolas Jenson (see *B2*).

This book is nicely printed. Generous margins have been allowed (even though the marginal note on folio 13v shows that this copy has been cropped in rebinding), and the type impression, though dark, is of a very even 'colour'.

In order to condense the text, and to aid the justifying of the lines, numerous 'shorthand' symbols and abbreviations, indicated by a tilde (~), are employed. This necessitated the casting of many extra 'sorts', far beyond the basic alphabet.

Note the blunt baseline serifs on the minims; the 'uncial' form of **h**; and the awkward-looking lower bowl of **g**. The more 'gothic' traits of this type can be seen in the extreme stress and 'square' shape of **o** and letters based on it, like **d** and **q**; and the rather angular arch forms of **a**, **m**, and **n**.

mihi sunt suspecta. Crassum quidem nostrum minore dignitate aiunt
profectum paludatum q̄ olim æqualem eius. L. Paulum. Item. T. Tetrū
consulem. O hominem neq̄. De libris oratoris factū est a me diligēter.
Diminutum quæ ī manibus fuerunt: describas lic&. Illud etiā te rogo
ne istuc hospes uenias. Vale.

M. T. C. A. S. xiii.

Nestorius noster me per litteras fecit certioré: te Roma ad octauū
idus maii putare profectum esse tardius q̄ dixerat: quod minus
ualuisses. Si iam melius uales uehementer gaudeo. Velim domum ad
tuos scribas: ut tibi tui libri pateant: non secus ac si ipse adesses cum
cæteri tū Varronis. Est eni mihi utēdum quibusdam rebus ex his libris
ad eos quos in manibus habeo: quos ut spero tibi ualde probabo. Veli
siq̄d forte noui habes: maxime a. Qu. fratre: deinde a. C. Cæsare: & siq̄d
de comitiis de re.p. (forte soles eni tu hæc festine odorari) cōscribas ad
me. Si nihil habebis tamen scribas aliq̄d. Nunq̄ eni mihi tua epistola
aut intempestiua aut loquax uisa est. maxime autem rogo rebus tuis:
totoq̄ itinere ex sententia confecto nos q̄primum reuisas. Dionysium
iube taluere. Cura ut ualeas. M. T. C. A. S. xiii.

De Eutychide gratum qui uetere prænomine nouo nomine Titus
erit Cecilius: ut ē ex me: & ex te uictus Dionysius. M. Pōponius
ualde mehercule mihi gratum si Eutychides tuā erga me bentuolentiā
cognoscē:&: suam illam in meo dolore neq̄ tum mihi
obscurā neq̄ post ingratam fuisse. Iter asiaticum tuum puto suscipiē-
dum fuisse. Nunq̄ enim tu sine iustissima causa tam lōga a tot tuis &
hōibus & rebus carissimis & suauissimis abesse uoluisses. Sed humai-
tātē tuā amoreq̄ ī tuos reditus celeritas declarauit. Sed uereor ne lepore
suo detinet diutius prætor Clodius & homo pereruditus ut aiunt: &
nunc quidem deditus græcis litteris ac pituaniis: sed si uis homo esse
recipe te ad nos ad quod tempus confirmasti: cum illis tum cum salui
uenerint Romæ uiuere licebit: auere te scribis accipere aliq̄d a me īraq̄.
Dedi ac multis quidem de rebus perscripta omīa: sed ut
conticio: quoniā non mihi uideris in Epiro diu fuisse redditas tibi nō
arbitor. Genus autē mearum ad te quidem litteraq̄ eiusmodi forte est:
ut non libeat cuiq̄ dare nisi de explorato sit tibi eum redditur.
Nunc romanas accipe res. Ad. iii. nonas quintiles Suffennas: & Cato
absoluti: Porcilius commēdatur: ex quo intellectum est tres
ambitum comitia interregnum maiestatem totam deniq̄ rempublicā
flocci nō facere: debemus patrēfamilias domi suæ occidere nolle: neq̄
tamen id ipsū abunde. Nā absoluerunt. xxxii. cōdemnauerunt. xxviii.

Italian Renaissance Types   *Nicolas Jenson*   B2

> ab ipſa cõmiſſione ad m
> omia reliquorum ludor
> us. Reliqua pars epiſtol
> erdum iacit igniculos u
> pretari miſi ad te exemj

Chicago, The Newberry Library, INC. 4064. Cicero, *Epistolae ad Brutum*. Printed in Venice, Italy in 1470.

The page size is 12⅞" x 9" (327 x 230 mm). (A rebinding in the 17th century cropped the margins, especially the head.) The text measure is 5⅜" (137 mm). The book has 182 folios. The whole-page reproduction is taken from folio 65R, the enlargement (four times actual size) from folio 165V.

Nicolas Jenson was born at Sommevoire, in Burgundy in northern France *c.* 1420. He was trained as a goldsmith, possibly at Tours. His familiarity with metal casting at a very small scale must have served him well as he learned the craft of punchcutting and typefounding. He spent a little time in Germany before he moved to Venice, and it is possible that he actually met Johann Gutenberg in Frankfurt.

However, Jenson was not the very first printer in Venice. Johann von Speyer (Giovanni da Spira) had already printed Cicero's *Epistolae ad familiares* there in 1469, using a roman type which may well have been cut for him by Jenson.

In Mainz, printers had naturally taken contemporary German manuscript hands as the basis for their typeforms, so it is not surprising that, when the art of printing arrived in Italy, the typefounders there copied the humanist minuscule of renaissance scribes. Jenson's letterforms bear great similarity to Italian manuscripts of his day. (See *Historical Scripts, F4* written about the same time as this Cicero was printed.)

Interestingly, for the majority of the 150 books he printed in the ten years until his death in 1480, Jenson used five different gothic rotunda founts. But this roman type (the same one that he used for his 1470 edition of Eusebius' *De evangelica praeparatione*) has been greatly admired and has been the inspiration for many modern typefaces.

Jenson's pages are extremely austere. Just one size of type is used throughout, and capitals are merely used as initials – a few hand-written capitals offer the only relief. But the type is skilfully cut. Its consistency of form, accurate alignment, and close fitting result in very legible (if Latin!) text.

Jenson's capitals follow classical Roman inscriptional letter shapes and proportions, though some of them, like **D**, **H**, **N**, and **S**, are rather wide and are as tall as the ascenders. Note the double-seriffed top of **M**, and the very rare **K** (in the enlargement above).

The lowercase letters have an unmistakable calligraphic character. The strokes of a broad pen can be sensed underlying many of Jenson's forms – note the terminals at the top of **a** and **f**; the slightly angular bowls of **d**, **p**, **q**, and **a**; and the natural scribal axis for the tilted crossbar of **e** (in places, with a tiny 'pen' extension). The tiny dot on **i** is offset, perhaps to avoid a clash with **f** and **ſ** (see **ffi**, line 1 above). This is the first use in type of a non-'uncial' form of **h**.

> noui habes:maxime a. Qu. fratre:deind

placet); sicuti matres filiorum nomina, qui desyderantur, in eos saepe transfferunt, quos habent; ita et nos Platanos illas uocemus. B. P. Mihi uero placet illas populos semper uocari: atq; haud scio, an etiam cum eas tempestas ue tustásue consumpserit (ut ait ille de quercu Mariana), tamen erit in Noniano populus, quam Bembeam populum uocét: ita mihi quidem uidetur illas aeternitati cómendasse suis carminibus Aurelius noster. Quare;
Quae uitreas populus arduo
Bembeas ad aquas uertice tollitur
Viuum cespitem obumbrans,
Intonsa bicolor coma
sit semper populus: crescat; surgat altius uel aquila ista, uel poetae uersu: sed (ut ad Platanos redeam) non tá mea causa istud ipsum cupiebá fili, q̃ tua: ego enim me oblectaui satis; tũ experiendo illud didici, ut nequid admirarer: neq; si quid sero

Italian Renaissance Types   *Aldus Manutius*   B3

[Enlarged specimen of type reading: "o insculpta; sed in argen / um; quod etiam Syracu / t ferè per totam insulam / in coctile theatrum adhu / id, quod Romae uidi"]

Chicago, The Newberry Library, INC. 5550. Pietro Bembo, *De Aetna*. Printed in Venice, Italy, by Aldus Manutius in 1496.

The page size is 7¾" x 5½" (196 x 140 mm). (The margins have probably been trimmed.) The text measure is 3" (76 mm). The book has 30 folios. The whole-page reproduction is taken from folio 9v, the enlargement (four times actual size) from folio 7v.

Although Aldus Manutius is one of the most honoured names in typographic history – he is considered *the* scholar-printer of the Italian Renaissance (learned in Greek, Latin, and probably also Hebrew) – he was not a punchcutter and probably never operated a printing press himself.

Teobaldo Mannucci (which he himself Latinised as 'Aldus Manutius Romanus') was born *c.* 1451 not far from Rome, in the small town of Bassiano. Apparently, he studied in both Rome and Ferrara, and from 1480 was tutor to two young princes of Carpi.

He arrived in Venice in the summer of 1490. Once settled there he wrote a Latin Grammar, and in 1493 he had it published by Andrea Torresani who was an established printer in Venice. Within two years Aldus had set up his own printing company with Torresani and Pierfrancesco Barbarigo as financial backers.

Aldus' primary aim for his newly-established 'Aldine' Press was to publish the Greek classics. Whilst Venice excelled in the printing of books in Latin at that time, very little printing of Greek works had been done previously. But Aldus was embarking on an extremely risky venture – the demand for texts in Greek was quite small, and the technical difficulties in making Greek type were considerable. Despite these obstacles, Aldus published his first book in February 1495, a Greek Grammar with Latin translation.

His first book solely in Latin was the little gem shown here, the *De Aetna* of 1496 containing memoirs of a trip to Sicily by the young Venetian poet Pietro Bembo. The delicate roman type cut by Francesco Griffo (see *B5*) contrasts with the earlier, heavier letterforms of Nicolas Jenson *(B2)*. Griffo's capitals are in better harmony with the lowercase than Jenson's, being somewhat shorter than the ascenders. But note the peculiar **M** (lines 4 and 8) with no serif at the top right; the rather long leg on the **R**; and the **i** with the tiny dot shifted to the right. Some variant letterforms were cut, like the very strange **p**, more like a capital form, (see line 5, po**p**ulos), and a few others (like **a**, **e**, **m**, **r**, and **t** with added flourish) not actually shown on this page.

This typeface is famous as the inspiration for Robert Estienne's new types of 1530 (see *C2* notes), for the 20th-century 'revivals' of Monotype *Bembo* (1929), and for the even closer copy by Giovanni Mardersteig, called *Griffo*.

[Specimen: "cōmendasse suis carminibus Aurelius no"]

SACRATISSIMO CAESA-
RI MAXIMILIANO ROMA
NORVM REGI AVGVSTIS
SIMO IOANNES FRANCI
SCVS PICVS MIRANDV-
LAE DOMINVS, CON-
CORDIAEQVE
COMES.

Scribit Eusebius Pamphili summe Regum Maximiliane Auguste, uideri sibi gentium philosophos, si aut inter se, aut cum aliis compararet, claros illos quidem uiros fuisse, si uero eos ipsos philosophis, theologisq; conferret, qui ueri dei cultui uacassent, inanes, & friuolos, Sic mihi de te fari liceat Augustissime Cæsar. Visi n. summa & æstimatiõe & gloria digni multi, qui hunc, quem tu felicissime insides Romani imperii thronum conscendere, si uel inter sese, uel aliis cum regibus diuersarum gentium, & nationum cõferantur,

Parma, Biblioteca Palatina, LL VII 8. Giovanni Francesco Pico, *Liber de imaginatione*. Printed in Venice, Italy by Aldus Manutius in 1501.

The page size is 7⅝" x 5¼" (194 x 134 mm). The text measure is 3" (76 mm). The book has 112 pages. The whole-page reproduction is taken from page 10, the enlargement (four times actual size) from page 11.

Aldus Manutius continued to use the *De Aetna* types (see B3) for other important books he published. He did, however, rethink the capitals. Lighter, more elegant forms were cut for him by Francesco Griffo, and they first appeared in his books from July 1499. The lowercase of *De Aetna* and the new capitals were used for the now famous *Hypnerotomachia Poliphili*, with its very stylish layout and magnificent woodcuts, which he published in December of that year.

Giovanni Mardersteig, in his Introduction to a facsimile of *De Aetna* (published by the Officina Bodoni in 1969), claimed that not only were the capitals replaced for *Hypnerotomachia Poliphili*, but also the lowercase letters. However, recent detailed digital comparisons by Riccardo Olocco have proved that, contrary to Mardersteig's assertion, the lowercase used for *Hypnerotomachia Poliphili* is exactly the same as that used for *De Aetna*. What is different is the letter *spacing*. This change began to happen, progressively, in the books printed by Aldus from 1497 onwards. Surprisingly, for such a carefully designed work, the quality of the printed text in *Hypnerotomachia Poliphili* is poor. The type seems badly worn, and it is unevenly inked, which is perhaps why Mardersteig was convinced that Aldus used different, rougher type for *Hypnerotomachia Poliphili*.

The book illustrated here was also printed by Aldus and was published in April of 1501. It uses the same type, both capitals and lowercase, that was used for *Hypnerotomachia Poliphili*, but the print quality here is much fresher – apparently the same fount was newly cast.

De imaginatione, despite its small format and simple design, is an elegant book. Its spacious margins enhance the carefully considered typesetting, and the beautifully proportioned capitals provide a nicely judged contrast with the lowercase text. The capitals, with their very open spacing and striking *diminuendo*, are reminiscent of classic inscriptional letters of ancient Rome.

Griffo's new capitals are indeed lighter in weight, and more refined than those he cut for *De Aetna*. **A** and **N** are wider; the top of **M** has serifs on both sides; but **A** retains its flat top, and **R** its long leg. Note the elegant **g** with its angled lower bowl. The few flourished lowercase letters included in *De Aetna* are now discarded, and there are very few ligatures, just ff, ﬄ, and ft. The ﬁ pair has probably been kerned.

31

Ch'interrompendo di mia vita il corso
M'han facto habitator d'ombroso bosco:
Rendimi, s'esser po, libera & sciolta
L'errante mia consorte: & fia tuo'l pregio;
S'anchor teco la troua in miglior parte.
Hor ecco in parte le question mie noue;
S'alcun pregio in me viue, o in tutto è corso,
O l'alma sciolta, o ritenuta al bosco.

SONETTO CLXXX

In nobil sangue vita humile & queta,
Et in alto intellecto vn puro core;
Fructo senile in sul giouenil fiore,
E in aspecto pensoso anima lieta
Raccolto ha in questa donna el suo pianeta:
Anzi'l re de le stelle; e'l vero honore,
Le degne lode, e'l gran pregio, e'l valore;
Ch'è da stancar ogni diuin poeta.
Amor s'è in lei con honestate aggiunto;
Con belta naturale habito adorno,
Et vn acto, che parla con silentio;
Et non so che ne gli occhi; ch'in vn punto
Po far chiara la nocte, oscuro il giorno,
E'l mel amaro, & addolcir l'assentio.

SONETTO CLXXXI

Tutto'l di piango; & poi la nocte, quando
Prendon riposo i miseri mortali,
Trouom'in pianto, & raddopiansi i mali:
Cosi spendo'l mio tempo lachrimando.

m ii

Italian Renaissance Types   *Francesco Griffo   B5*

Chicago, The Newberry Library, Wing zp 535 .s7023. Francesco Petrarch, *Opere.* Printed in Fano, Italy by Gershom Soncino in 1503.

The page size is 6⅛" x 3¾" (156 x 96 mm). The overall text measure is 2⅜" (61 mm). The book has 200 folios. The whole-page reproduction is taken from folio m ii(r), the enlargement (five and a half times actual size) from folio o vi(r).

The first appearance of an italic typeface, in the Virgil published by Aldus Manutius in 1501, was a remarkable innovation. Today, we tend to think of italic as an *adjunct* to roman: a compressed, sloping letterform used to provide emphasis or contrast within roman text. But the first italic fount was conceived as a stand-alone face, designed for a series of Latin classics published in a new, small format.

Aldus explained that these *'libelli portaliles'*, were printed 'in our small fount, so that you may carry it conveniently with you as a travelling companion'. This new series of books had three distinguishing features – the small, rather narrow, format (one copy of the Virgil measures just 6½" x 3⅞", 164 x 99 mm); a plain but carefully edited text (omitting the usual commentaries and glosses); and an unprecedented typeface (the new, tiny italic). In the colophon of the 1501 Virgil, Aldus pays tribute to the engraver of this type – *'scalpta daedaleis Francisci manibus Bononiensis'* (cut by the skilled hands of Francis of Bologna). This punchcutter has now been firmly identified as Francesco Griffo.

Shortly after the completion of the Virgil, Griffo quarrelled with Aldus and moved to a rival printer, Gershom Soncino. For printing the Petrarch illustrated here, Griffo cut a second italic type, even better than the italic he made for Aldus. In the dedication, Soncino praises Griffo's punchcutting skill, but he also takes a sideswipe at Aldus, strongly implying that he was now attempting to take the credit for Griffo's work. 'Francesco is not only able to cut the standard types but he has invented a new kind of letter, called cursive or *cancellaresca*. He – and not Aldus Romanus or others who have cleverly tried to borrow his plumes – is the original inventor and designer. He cut all the types used by this Aldus.'

Despite the small size of Griffo's italic type, he retains many of the cursive features of handwriting. Note the use of upright capitals, shorter than the ascenders; the alternate forms of **d**, **p**, **q**, **s**, and the playful **z**; and the many scribal ligatures like ᶜt, fa, fi, ǫu, ſp, ff, and ft. Note also the unusual **a** and the two forms of ampersand, *&*. The cutting of the first italic type on a rectangular body (with its sloping letterforms and flowing extenders) was a technical triumph.

33

POET. LIB. II

Sæpe suis subito inuenient accommoda uotis,
Altera nempe arti tantum est obnoxia cura,
Vnde solent laudem imprimis optare poetæ.
Vestibulum ante ipsum, primoque in lumine semper
Prudentes leuiter rerum fastigia summa
Libant, et parcis attingunt omnia dictis,
Quæ canere statuere, simul cœlestia Diuum
Auxilia implorant propriis nil uiribus ausi.
Quos ores autem non magni denique refert,
Dum memor auspiciis cuiusquam cuncta Deorum
Aggrediare. Iouis neque enim nisi rite uocato
Numine fas quicquam ordiri mortalibus altum.
Nec sat opem implorare semel musasque ciere.
Sed quoties ueluti scopuli durissima dictu
Obiicient sese tibi non superanda labore
Mortali, diuos toties orare licebit.
Incipiens odium fugito, facilesque legentum
Nil tumidus demulce animos, nec grandia iam tum
Conuenit, aut nimium cultum ostentantia fari.
Omnia sed nudis prope erit fas promere uerbis.

C

Italian Renaissance Types   *Ludovico degli Arrighi   B6*

Chicago, The Newberry Library, WING ZP 535 .L965. Marco Girolamo Vida, *De arte poetica.* Printed in Rome, Italy in May 1527.

   The page size is 9" x 5½" (230 x 140 mm). The overall text measure is 3⅜" (85 mm). The book has 111 folios. The whole-page reproduction is taken from folio C i(R), the enlargement (five times actual size) from folio E iiii(R).

Arrighi, also known as Ludovico Vicentino, is most famous as the author of two handwriting manuals, *La Operina* and *Il modo de temperare le penne*, composed in 1522 and 1523. He was a professional scribe who wrote manuscripts for prominent men of his day, like Giulio de' Medici, and was appointed scribe in the Vatican Chancery from about 1515. In 1522 he moved to Venice and set up his own printing establishment, transferring it when he returned to Rome in 1526. Altogether he printed and published at least 27 titles whilst in Venice, and a further ten in Rome. He was probably killed in May 1527 when the armies of Charles V attacked Rome, and some 4000 citizens perished.

   While there has been endless debate regarding the scribal exemplar for the 1501 italic type of Aldus/Griffo (many inconclusive suggestions have been made), it is quite obvious that Arrighi's italic types, with their long ascenders and descenders, were a skilful adaptation of his own *cancellaresca corsiva* script (see *Historical Scripts, B6)*. But he did not make the type himself, the superb punches were cut for him by Lautizio Perugino, a goldsmith.

   There has been some confusion as to exactly how many typefaces Arrighi designed, some claiming as many as six, but A S Osley (1965) has convincingly argued that Arrighi made just two basic founts, each with many variant forms.

   This Vida is printed with Arrighi's second, more restrained, italic type; a great improvement on Griffo's version *(B5)*. Gian Giorgio Trissino, author of a book printed by Arrighi in 1524, summed it up: 'Just as in handwriting (Arrighi) has excelled all our contemporaries, so, with this fine new invention for executing with the printing press almost everything which he used to do with his pen, he has beaten every other printer with his beautiful type.'

   Arrighi's consummate calligraphic expertise can be discerned not only in the assured way his written forms have been translated into type, but also in his elegant *mise-en-page* – the interlinear spaces are wide and page margins generous. Note that there are no abbreviations at all, just a few ligatures: ct, ff, st *and* ft, and the unusual **gg**. Note also the wide **x** and the heavy, lozenge-shaped full point.

DIVI IOANNIS CHRY
SOSTOMI LIBER CONTRA GENTILES
Babylæ episcopi ac martyris vitam continens,
Germano Brixio Altissiodoren. interprete.

Ominus noster IESVS ad crucis sup
plicium iamiam accessurus, ac mor=
tem illam viuificam moriturus, illa
ipsa nocte postrema, dum discipu=
los ad se suos semotis arbitris vocas=
set, apud eos quum permulta verba
alia fecit, eosdem plurimarum rerum cõmonefaciẽs,
tum inter alia, & tale quiddã ad eos locutus est. Amen
amen dico vobis, qui credit in me, opera quæ ego fa=
cio, & ille faciet, & his maiora faciet. Atqui multi o=
lim alij magistri extitere, qui & discipulos habuerũt,
& miracula item ostentarunt, quemadmodum iacti=
tantes gloriantur gentiles, verũtamen illorum nemo
vnquam eiusmodi orationem vsurpare, ac ne animo
quidem versare ausus est. neq3 sane possint è gentili=
bus aliqui, etiam si nullius illos mendacij pudeat, com
mõstrare huiusmodi elogium, sermonémve apud se
extare. spectra quidem certe demortuorum, neq3 nõ
cadauerum quorundam simulachra qui repræsenta=
rent, multi multos apud se nouarum, mirandarúmq3

b.j.

Bern, Universitätsbibliothek, UB ZB BONG I 25:7. Johannes Chrysostomus, *Liber contra gentiles*. Printed in Paris, France by Simon de Colines in 1528.

The page size is 7¾" x 5⅝" (197 x 143 mm). The text measure is 3¾" (95 mm). The book has 72 folios. The whole-page reproduction is taken from folio b i(R), the enlargement (four times actual size) from folio A i(R).

In about 1522 Simon de Colines married Guyonne Viart, the widow of the renowned Parisien printer, Henri Estienne. He thus became step-father to Estienne's sons, including Robert (see *C2)*, and also to Guyonne's children from a yet previous marriage. When Henri died in 1520, Colines became the director of the Estienne Press (also Latinised as the 'Stephanus' Press). After Robert Estienne took over the Press in 1526, Colines moved his own operation to another workshop in the same street, the rue Saint-Jean-de-Beauvais.

He was a prolific printer, publishing more than 700 titles up to the time of his death in 1546. Simon de Colines is regarded as the finest typographer in Paris during the 1520s, admired for the outstanding quality of his printing, and an inspiration for many others in what was to become the Golden Age of French printing.

While the evidence is only circumstantial that Colines himself cut the types used by the Estienne Press in the early days, Vervliet (2008) cites 16th-century French writers who praise the 'elegance and beauty' of Colines' letters and his skill in 'the art of cutting type', and he also refers to Guillaume Le Bé II, who in both the *Inventory* of *c.* 1618 and the *Memorandum* of *c.* 1643 records certain types 'cut by Colines'. All of the 19 roman types attributed to Colines by Vervliet (2010) were used solely by the Estienne family presses, so it is very likely indeed that they were produced 'in-house', and by Colines himself.

This example is an assured *gros-romain* (*c.* 16.5pt) type from the beginning of Simon de Colines' mature period. The clarity of the printed type is enhanced by the beautifully balanced *mise-en-page*, large margins, and careful arrangement of the different sizes of type. However, compared to the later types of Estienne and Garamont in the '*De Aetna*' style (see *C2* notes), these letterforms are 'dark', and the ascenders and descenders are comparatively short, creating close line spacing. Overall, it is somewhat reminiscent of the Jenson 'Eusebius' type of 1470 (see *B2*). For example, the capitals are heavy and about the same height as the short ascenders, the lowercase letters **o**, **b**, **d**, **p**, and **q** are very round, and **e** has the tilted crossbar typical of humanist minuscule scripts. After 1530 Colines actually modified his type, making it a little lighter, more like the '*De Aetna*' style.

Note the **g** with large bowls; **j** (used as the second letter of 'double i'); the point of the **v** which drops below the baseline; and the decorative lozenge-shaped full point.

Ad eoſdem literæ ſe-
RENISSIMORVM EIVSDEM RE-
gis liberorum.

FRANCISCVS Dei gratia, Chriſtianiſſimi Galliarũ Regis primogenitus Delphinus Viennenſis ac Britanniæ Dux,&c. Henricus Aurelianorum, & Carolus Engoliſmorum Duces, &c. eiuſdem Chriſtianiſſimi Regis etiam filii: Reuerẽdiſſimis, illuſtriſſimis, generoſis, magnificis & ſpectabilibus ſacri Romani Imperii ordinibus, conſanguineis, amicis, & fœderatis chariſſimis s.

GVLIELMO Bellaio Lãgii domino Chriſtianiſſimi Regis patris, ac domini noſtri ſemper obſeruãdi conſiliario & intimo cubiculario, ad vos de arduis ac magnis rebus nũc Legato, quædam etiam ad vos mãdata communiter dedimus, super hæreditariis quibuſdã noſtris rationibus: quarũ nomine quum eiuſdem ſacri Rom. Imperii beneficiarii & clientes ſimus, viſum eſt nobis, apud alios quàm apud veſtros ipſos ampliſſimos ordines conqueri non de-

French Renaissance Types — *Robert Estienne I   C2*

> vniuerſa reſpub. verè Chr
> vos, amici, deſyderetis.
> ſimi, inclyti, generoſi, ſplē
> les, & prudētes, amici, ſoci
> eum Optimū Maximum

Chicago, The Newberry Library, CASE F 3919 .314. [François I], *Exemplaria literarum*. Printed in Paris, France in 1537.

The page size is 7½" x 5¾" (193 x 147 mm). The text measure is 3⅝" (92 mm). The book has 216 pages. The whole-page reproduction is taken from page 137, the enlargement (four times actual size) from page 197.

Robert Estienne I is considered to be one of the most eminent French scholar-printers of the 16th century, very much on a par with Aldus Manutius of Venice (see *B3* notes). In 1539 he was appointed *imprimeur du roi* (printer of Latin and Hebrew for François I) as successor to Conrad Néobar. The next year he was also appointed as printer of Greek. Estienne later edited, printed, and published erudite works – his corrections to the text of the Latin Vulgate Bible in fact brought him into conflict with Catholic authorities in France. As a scholar Estienne is perhaps best-known for his *Thesaurus linguae latinae*, but his French Bible of 1533 was the very first to number the verses – an innovation of lasting significance, taken for granted today.

In 1530 Estienne introduced a remarkable set of roman types which profoundly influenced contemporary French typography. Up to this time, he had been using a heavier, less-refined, and somewhat archaic type inherited from his step-father, Simon de Colines (see *C1*). The new types were unprecedented. They were the first types to be produced as *a series* in wide range of sizes, from a *gros-canon* (roughly 42pt) to a minute *nonpareille* (approx 6pt). The *gros-canon* was the very first complete upper and lowercase to be produced at such a large size. The five types were deliberately matching. Undoubtedly they were all based on the same model – their lightness of weight, refinement of detail, and overall style were quite clearly copied from the Aldine *De Aetna* typeface of 1495 (see *B3*), even down to the peculiar single-seriffed **M** and the off-centre dot on the i!

Previously, it has been widely presumed that these elegant roman types were the work of Claude Garamont. However, Vervliet (2008, 2010) has convincingly argued that, by 1530, Garamont would have been too young and too inexperienced to have made these. The only other notable punchcutter in Paris, Simon de Colines, had established his own press by then. Instead, Vervliet suggests that a certain 'Maître Constantin' (mentioned in the Le Bé *Memorandum* of c. 1643, alongside de Colines and Augereau), as the most likely candidate.

This page shows the *gros-romain* size (*c.* 16.5pt) from this series of 1530 Estienne types. Note the close similarity with the *De Aetna* typeface *(B3)* – for example, the 'cupped' apex of **A**; the inward serif on the upright of **G**; the single-seriffed **M**; the off-centre dot on the **i**; the low point of the **v**. Overall, the capitals are nicely balanced with the lowercase; not quite as tall as the ascenders.

> quibuſdā noſtris rationibus: quarū nomi

Philopœmen.

A tenance que le font ordinairement ceulx qui en cause de si grand dueil, ne si esiouir que ceulx qui uenoiét de gaigner une si gráde uictoire. Ceulx des uilles, bourgs & uillages de dessus le chemin uenoient au deuant pour toucher à la buye de ses cédres, ne plus ne moins qu'ils luy souloiét toucher en la main & le caresser quand il retournoit de quelque guerre, & accompagnoient son conuoy iusques à la uille de Megalopolis: à l'entree de laquelle se trouuerét les uieilles gens auec les femmes & les enfans, qui se meslans parmy les gens de guerre renouuellerent les pleurs, regrets & lamentations de toute la miserable uille, laquelle estimoit auoir perdu quant & son citoien le premier lieu d'honneur en la communaulté des Achéens. Si fut inhumé comme il luy appartenoit fort honorablement, & furét les prisonniers de Messine tous assommez à coups de pierre à l'entour de sa sepulture. Toutes les uilles de l'Achaie entre plusieurs autres honneurs qu'elles luy decernerent, luy feirent dresser des images à sa semblàce: mais depuis au malheureux temps de la Grece, quád la uille de Corinthe fut arse & destruitte par les Romains, il y eut un calûniateur Romain, qui s'efforcea de les faire toutes abbattre, le chargeát & l'accusant, comme s'il eust esté en uie, d'auoir esté tousiours ennemy des Romains, & mal affectionné à la prosperité de leurs affaires: mais apres que Polybius luy eut respondu, ny le Consul Mummius ny ses assesseurs & lieutenans ne uou-

C lurent permettre que lon abolist les hóneurs faits à la memoire d'un si excellent personnage, combien qu'il eust en plusieurs choses nuit & à Titus Quintius, & à Manius. Mais ces gens de bien là, mettoient difference entre le deuoir & le profit, & estimoiét estre choses distinctes & separees l'une de l'autre, que l'honnesté & l'utilité, ainsi comme le droit & la raison le ueulent aussi, aians opinion que tout ainsi comme ceulx qui reçoiuent des bienfaits sont tenus d'en rendre la pareille à leurs bienfaicteurs, & leur en doiuent la recognoissance: aussi aux hommes de uertu toutes gens de bien doiuent honneur & reuerence. Voila quant à la uie de Philopœmen.

Titus Quintius Flaminius.

D IL est aisé à ueoir de quelle forme & stature estoit Titus Quintius Flaminius, que nous apparions à Philopœmen, par une statue de cuyure faitte à sa semblàce, qui est encore auiourdhuy à Rome aupres du gràd Apollo, qui fut apporté de Carthage, assis tout droit deuant l'entree des lices, & y a soubz laditte statue une inscription en lettres Grecques: Mais quant à ses meurs & son naturel, on dit qu'il estoit prompt & soudain, tant
E à courroucer, cóme à faire plaisir, diuersement toutefois: car s'il chastioit quelcun à qui il fust courroucé, il le faisoit legerement, & ne tenoit point son courroux: & au contraire, ses bienfaits estoient gráds, & si demouroit tousiours bien affectionné enuers ceulx à qui il auoit une fois fait plaisir, ne plus ne moins que s'il eulx mesmes luy en eussent fait, estát tousiours prest à faire de rechef en mieulx pour ceulx qui luy estoient redeuables, à fin de les entretenir & garder tousiours en sa deuotion, comme la plus belle acquisition qu'il eust sceu faire. Et pource qu'il estoit conuoiteux de gloire &

French Renaissance Types   *Claude Garamont   C3*

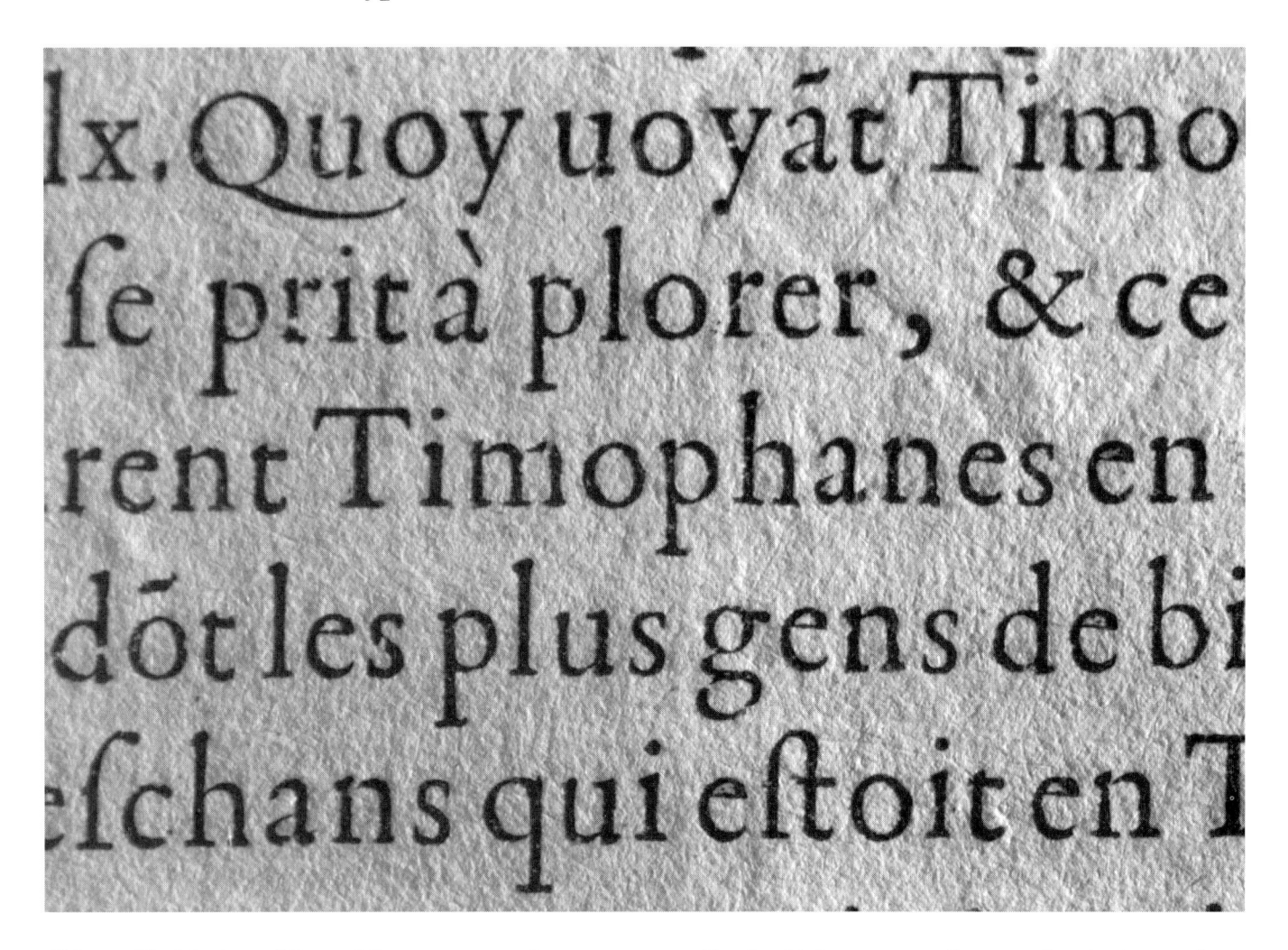

Chicago, The Newberry Library, WING ZP 539 .v478. Plutarch, *Les vies des hommes illustres.* Printed in Paris, France by Michel de Vascosan, in May 1559.

The page size is 14¾" x 9½" (375 x 242 mm). The text measure is 6⅛" (157 mm). The book has 734 pages. The whole-page reproduction is taken from page 258, the enlargement (four times actual size) from page 179.

In his will of 1549 Jean de Gagny, chancellor of the University of Paris, described Claude Garamont as 'the best letter-engraver in Paris'. History has confirmed his opinion.

By 1530, Paris had supplanted Venice as the pre-eminent publishing centre of Europe. It was producing books of the highest quality and its printing types were unrivalled. The elegant roman types of Garamont largely contributed to that achievement. There were many accomplished punchcutters in Paris at that time, but Garamont with Granjon *(C4)*, stood head and shoulders above them all.

Apart from a very short-lived venture into publishing from 1545–1546, Garamont's working life was as an independent maker of types, supplying printers with his superbly crafted founts. While he was not known as an innovator, he refined the best of what had gone before. His types were skilfully cut and elegantly designed. He was prolific; at least 34 different types have been attributed to him, 17 romans, 7 italics, 8 greeks, and 2 hebrews.

Despite this large output, Garamont has, in the past, been credited with types he did *not* cut – not only the 1530 Estienne Romans (see *C2* notes), but also the *Caractères de l'Université* first seen in 1621 (see *D1* notes). It was not until 1926 that Paul Beaujon (Beatrice Warde) recognised them as the types of Jean Jannon. Unfortunately, by then, many modern type foundries had already produced representations of 'Garamond' types, mistakenly basing them on Jannon's *Caractères de l'Université*. To this day, *most* typefaces called 'Garamond' are really copies of Jannon! An exception is the fine 'Adobe Garamond' by Robert Slimbach that you are now reading.

The book shown here, *Les vies des hommes*, handsomely printed by Michel de Vascosan, makes the most of Garamont's *gros-romain* (*c.* 16.5pt) type. This is a beautifully-designed fount, having very even 'colour' (no single letter obtrudes) and excellent alignment – a masterpiece of restraint. The well-balanced capitals are shorter than the tall ascenders. Note that there are no abbreviations used, except for the ampersand (&). Note also the leg of the **R** which falls just below the baseline, and the very long, elegant tail on the **Q**.

OPPIANI DE VENATIONE
LIBER SECVNDVS.

Eia Iouis proles pedibus nitidißima Phœbe,
Vna cum Phœbo uitales missa sub auras,
Fascia cui cingit flauos aurata capillos:
Dic mihi qui primus per inhospita tesqua ferarum
Heroúmue hominúmue tuas exercuit artes?
Centauri, crudele genus, prolésque biformis,
Ventosæ Pholoës, cliuis utrinque recuruæ,
Portentosi homines ad lumbos usque, sed ultra
Cornipedum formas immania terga figurant,
Venandi ingenuas artes reperiße feruntur.
Inter mortales primùm auricomo Ioue cretus
Perseus, qui gladio ceruicem Gorgonis hausit.
Præpetibus siquidem pennis abreptus in auras,
A latis pedibus capras capiebat agrestes,
Et thoas, ceruos, oryges, damásque, lupósque,
Lucifer inuenit uenatus Castor equestres.
Nanque feras trepidas partim confecit acerbis.
Transadigens telis, partímque per auia lustra
Cœpit equis agitans leuibus, cursúque fatigans.
At Lacedæmonius generoso à sanguine Pollux,
Sæua canum genera in mauortia bella ferarum
Armauit, crudáque ferox certando palæstra,
Insandos homines occìdit: primus hic omnem
Edocuit superare feram, & captare molossis.
Acribus effulsit consertis comminus armis
Per syluas bello clarus Calydonius heros.

D iij

Chicago, The Newberry Library, CASE Y 642 .0635. Oppianus, *De venatione*. Printed in Paris, France by Michel de Vascosan, in 1555.

The page size is 8⅞" x 6¼" (225 x 157 mm). The overall text measure is 4" (102 mm). The book has 110 pages. The whole-page reproduction is taken from page 11, the enlargement (four and a half times actual size) from page 20.

Despite Claude Garamont's fame and reputation, actually very little is known of his life, especially of his early years. The Le Bé *Memorandum* (*c.* 1643), which is a series of short biographies of Parisien typographers of the 16th and early 17th centuries, provides otherwise unknown insights into the life and career of Garamont. But it was compiled almost 100 years after the events it records, and so is often unreliable – like the assertion that Garamont *completed* his apprenticeship with Antoine Augereau as early as 1510.

Vervliet (2008, 2010) has convincingly argued that it is much more likely that Garamont was *born* in 1510; that his apprenticeship probably lasted from *c.* 1525 until December 1534 when Augereau was executed for his Protestant faith; and that Garamont's mature productive period was from *c.* 1540 until his death in October or November 1561.

Of some things we *can* be sure. On 2 November 1540 Garamont was commissioned to furnish punches for a series of greek types for François I (the now-famous *grecs du roi* types). This contract was administered by Pierre Duchâtel,

counsellor and almoner of the King, and supervised by the *imprimeur du roi*, Robert Estienne I *(C2)*.

We also know that Guillaume Le Bé I (the father of the compiler of the 1643 *Memorandum*, mentioned in *C1* and *C2*) was trained in punchcutting at the Estienne Press, and actually worked with Garamont from 1551 until the latter's death in 1561. At that time, Le Bé I made an inventory of Garamont's estate and obtained a large quantity of Garamont's typographical materials for his own foundry.

Garamont's italics were never quite as popular as those of Granjon *(C4)*, yet this example of his *gros-romain* size of type (*c.* 16.5 pt) is very well-designed and skilfully cut. Note the consistent slope in the lowercase letters, but the use of broad, upright capitals, even within the text. The cursive character of the italic type is emphasised by the use of many 'scribal' ligatures including **ff, fl, fi, fp, fs, ff, st, ft**, and the linking of **as, is, us**. Note the long curving tail of **y** (undercutting the previous letter), and the elegant ampersand, *&*.

LIBER XXV. 441

EPITOME LIBRI XXV.

P. Cornelius Scipio, postea Africanus, ante legitimos annos ædilis factus est. Annibal vrbem Tarentum præter ciuem per Tarentinos tamen, qui se noctu venaturos simulauerunt, cepit. Ludi Apollinares ex Martij carminibus, quibus Cumensis clades prædicta fuerat, instituti sunt. T. Q. Fuluio & Ap. Claudio Coss. eburisi Hannonem Tiberium Gracchum prospere pugnauit. T. Sempronius Gracchus procos. ad Beneuentum insidiis inductus à Magone interemptus est. Centenius Penula, cui centuria militem acceperat à senatu, cum petisset à senatu, vt sibi exercitus daretur, pulsus caesusq́; esset, sibi ve imperabit, ee, ab amiculo viri fortis millessum acceperat militum dux fassus, conflixit cum Annibale, quum exercitus esset cæsus. Cn. Fuluius pr. mali exempli exemplum pugnaretur: in quo præliam ille esset cum militibus credidit, cum exercitus deuictus fuisset. Capua obsidebatur à Q. Fuluio, & Ap. Claudio Coss. Claudius Marcellus Syracusas expugnauit septimo anno, et ingressus in vrbem possit, in carmonitu vrbis capta. Arbitrandus iucretus forma quæ in puluere descripsit at, interfectus ibi. T. & Cn. Scipiones in Hispania post multas res bene gestas, vrtem feliciter gesserant in fortem ratum reliquere, propter cum tanta exercituum q́; eorum clades, quam in Hispania acciderat, amissi, ipsq́ue prouincia possessa sors. militi & Marrij cuiusdam hominis virtutis & industria contracto exercitus est, custoditu hortata, bina castra hostium expugnata essent, et dirriputa septem milia cæsa, ex inhelligere de predatione capta, dux Marcius appellatus est.

D VM hæc in Africa atque in Hispania geruntur, Annibal in agro Tarentino æstatem consumpsit, spe per proditionem vrbis Tarentinorum potiundæ. ipsorum interim Salentinorum ignobiles vrbes ad eum defecerunt. Eodem tempore in Bruttijs ex duodecim populis, qui anno priore ad Pœnos deficerant, Consentini & Thurini in fidem populi Romani redierunt. & plures redijssent, ni L. Pomponius Veientanus præfectus socium, prosperis aliquot populationibus in agro Bruttio iusti ducis speciem nactus, tumultuario exercitu coacto cum Hannone conflixisset. Magna ibi vis hominum, sed inconditæ turbæ agrestium seruorumq́ue cæsa aut capta est: minimumq́ue iacturæ fuit, quòd præfectus inter ceteros est captus, & tum temerariæ pugnæ author, & antè publicanus, omnibus malis artibus & Reipub. & societatibus infidus, damnosusq́ue. Sempronius Cos. in Lucanis multa prælia parua, haud vllum dignum memoratu fecit & ignobilia oppida Lucanorum aliquot expugnauit. Quo diutius trahebatur bellum, & variabant secundæ aduersæq́; res, nō fortunam magis quàm animos hominum : tanta religio, & ea magna ex parte externa, ciuitatem incesserat, vt aut homines, aut die repentè alij viderentur facti. nec iam in secreto modo atque intra parietes ac postes contemnebantur Romani ritus : sed in publico etiam ac foro Capitolioq́ue mulierum turba erat, nec sacrificantium nec precantium deos patrio more. Sacrificuli ac vates ceperant hominum mentes, quorum numerum auxit rustica plebs, ex incultis diutino bello infestisque agris egestate & metu in vrbem compulsa : & quæstus ex alieno errore facilis, quem velut ex concessæ artis vsu exercebant. Primò secreto bonorum indignationes exaudiebantur, deinde ad patres etiam, & ad publicam querimoniam excessit res. Incusati grauiter ab senatu ædiles triumuirique capitales, quod non prohiberent : cùm emouere eam multitudinem è foro, ac disijcere apparatus sacrorum conati essent, haud procul abfuit quin violarentur. Vbi potentius iam esse id malum apparuit, quàm vt minores per magistratus sedaretur: M. Aemylio Pr. vrbis negotium ab senatu datum est, vt & his religionibus populum liberaret. Is & in concione senatusconsultum recitauit, & edixit, vt quicunque libros vaticinos precationesue, aut artem sacrificandi conscriptam haberet, eos libros omnes literasque ad se ante Calendas Aprilis deferret : neu quis in publico sacroue loco, nouo aut externo ritu sacrificaret. Et aliquot publici sacerdotes mortui eo anno sunt: L. Cornelius Lentulus PONTIFEX MAXIMVS, & C. Papyrius C. F. Masso pontifex, & P. Furius Philus augur, & C. Papyrius, Lucius Fuluius Masso decemuir sacrorum. In Lentuli locum Marcus Cornelius

French Renaissance Types   *Robert Granjon*   C5

Cambridge, University Library, UL 1*.7.3-4(A). Livy, *Romanae historiae*. Printed in Frankfurt, Germany by George Corvinum, in May 1568.

The page size is 14½" x 9" (369 x 230 mm). The text measure is 6⅝" (168 mm). The book is in two volumes with a total of 1602 pages. The whole-page reproduction is taken from page 441, the enlargement (four times actual size) from page 9, both from volume one.

Paris, in the middle of the 16th century, was the acknowledged 'centre of excellence' for printing and typography. The craftsmen who supplied the type for this flourishing enterprise were numerous and skilful, but two punchcutters excelled – Claude Garamont, mainly for his elegant romans, and Robert Granjon for his italics of outstanding quality.

Although Granjon seemed to prefer making italics and other (even more exotic) faces, his later roman types in particular, such as the one shown here, were in fact superb. Stanley Morison (1967) considered them to be 'equal to Garamont's'. Praise indeed.

Born in Paris *c.* 1513, the son of a bookseller, Granjon nevertheless travelled a great deal as an itinerant punchcutter and spent time in many different cities – usually centres of printing and publishing like Lyons and Geneva, Antwerp and Frankfurt, as well as his home town of Paris. In Antwerp he worked with the printers Christophe Plantin and Willem Silvius. From 1578 he settled in Rome, continuing to make types (for the Vatican Press, among others) until 1589. He died in that city in 1590.

Granjon was the most prolific type maker of the 16th century. Vervliet attributes nearly 90 different typefaces to him, including 15 or so romans. This represents something like two complete sets of type each year during his active working life from *c.* 1543 to the late 1580s. His types were much sought-after by printers from many cities throughout Europe.

While in Antwerp in 1566, Plantin actually asked him to modify some types of Garamont. (Garamont had died in 1561.) He wanted to cast them on a smaller body size, so Granjon recut some of the punches, including Garamont's *cicéro* (*c.* 11.5pt) of 1552, shortening the ascenders and descenders of the lowercase letters.

This page from Livy's book printed in Frankfurt, shows Granjon's magnificent *gros-romain* (*c.* 16.5pt) type of 1566. Note the 'cupped' apex on **A**; the narrow style of **E**, **F**, **X**, and **Y**; the serifless tail of **K** and **R**; the slightly 'splayed' **M**; and the point of **v** extending below the baseline.

The original punches and matrices for this *gros-romain* type, and over 20 others by Granjon, are preserved in the Plantin-Moretus Museum in Antwerp, and some can also be seen in Stockholm and Oxford.

45

L'IMPRIMEVR AV LECTEVR.

Si pour mon commencement, Amy Lecteur, i'entreprens imprimer liures difficiles & de grands frais, cela ne me doit estre imputé à temerité ou folie, comme on faict communement à tous ceux qui me suiuent l'opinion depraucee des bons menagiers du temps present, qui disent. Qu'vn chascun doit auec peu de despence Acquerir biens qui soient de grand substance: car par l'institution qu'on m'a donnee depuis mon ieune aage, i'ay tousiours estimé que l'humaine felicité consistoit à employer pour le public: considerant plustost le proffit que la Republique pouoit rapporter de nostre labeur, que l'aquisition des grans biens & tresors du monde. Ainsi aussi ont vescu tous ceux qui ont voulu suiure la vertu, comme toutes histoires nous tesmoignent: & moy les desirant imiter, selon la vacation en laquelle il a pleu à Dieu m'appeller: m'estant presenté par maistre Iehan Cousin (en l'art de Portraicture & Peincture non infime à Zeusis, ou Apelles) vn liure de la pratique de Perspectiue, par luy composé, & les figures pour l'intelligence d'iceluy necessaires, portraittes de sa main sus planches de bois: i'ay accepté ladite offre, ay taillé la plus grand part desdittes figures, & quelques vnes qui au parauant estoient encommencees par maistre Aubin Oliuier, mon beau frere, les ay paracheuees, & mises en perfection, selon l'intention dudit Autheur: sçachant que le present liure donera instruction à vn million d'hommes de bien portraire toutes choses apres le naturel, sans trauail de corps & d'esprit, ains plustost auec grand contentement qui procedera de la raison, que trouueras dans cest œuure descrite. (e qui est chose de peu de pris, veu que si nous voulons considerer tout ce qui est soubz la concauité des cieux, nous confesserons la Portraiture estre mere & tutrice de touts arts, & de ce qui est digne de memoire. Cela nous tesmoigne assez Iosephus en son liure de la guerre des Iuifz, quand il parle de deux colomnes, l'vne de terre, & l'autre de cuiure, qui furent construittes par les filz d'Adam, auant le deluge, sur lesquelles les sept Arts Liberaux estoient descrits, insculpez, & leurs figures portraites. Les Egyptiens & Perses quand ils escriuoient, ils paignoient certains animaux par la propre nature desquels ils s'entendoient, comme s'ils eussent escrit selon nostre commun vsage. Et si on pourroit dire d'auantage, n'estoit que par le liure cognoistras cent fois plus que ie ne ti pourrois descrire. Et si ie cognois que ce mien premier coup d'essay te plaise, cela m'incitera d'imprimer choses vns de moindre importance & proffit. Parquoy à fin que m'excuses, me recommanderay à tes bonnes graces, & ce present liure aussi, lequel s'il te plaist, corrigeras à l'endroit où tu trouueras faute sans aucunement murmurer ne mesdire de ceux qui l'ont miz en lumiere. Et prieray Dieu, Amy Lecteur, te donner ce qui en luy tu desires.

Liure

French Renaissance Types   *Robert Granjon* C6

Chicago, The Newberry Library, Wing zp 539 .L565. Jean Cousin, *Livre de perspective.* Printed in Paris, France by Jean le Royer in 1560.

The page size is 15½" x 10⅜" (394 x 264 mm). The text measure is 6⅜" (163 mm). The book has 144 folios. The whole-page reproduction is taken from folio A iii(v), the enlargement (four times actual size) from A iii(r).

Despite the fact that Robert Granjon produced some very fine roman types (see *C4)*, he excelled in creating exotic styles like fancy italics and civilités. The latter were designed to look like handwriting, closely resembling the contemporary cursive Secretary Scripts. (For an example, see Michelle Brown, *Western Historical Scripts*, page 107.)

He cut a wide variety of italic types (nearly 30 of them). All of them were skilfully engraved and full of character, many with extravagant flourishes and swashes. He provided printers with a huge range of sizes from a minute *mignonne* of 1557 (*c.* 6.5pt) to a *gros-canon* (*c.* 42pt) of 1564. No other 16th-century punchcutter in France even attempted an italic of such a large size.

Vervliet distinguishes four stages in his italics – his early more hesitant attempts (1543–1550); a 'couché' period (from 1551) with the letters having a definite slope and a strong sense of style; then a 'droite' stage (1565–1570) where the letters were more upright and compact; and finally (1571–1579) a 'baroque' era incorporating rather spiky letters and lots of flourishes.

Granjon was the very first French type designer to incorporate *sloping* capitals with his italic lowercase (his *saint-augustin* of 1543). Early Italian 'chancery' italic types (see *B4, B5)* had retained upright capitals. Johann Singrener of Vienna was perhaps the first to slope italic capitals in type (1524), but of course sloping capitals in italic *manuscripts* were commonplace even in the 15th century. The famous Paduan scribe, Bartolomeo San Vito (1435– *c.* 1518) used them a great deal. Unlike earlier attempts, Granjon's sloping capitals are very well-balanced and harmonize completely with his lowercase.

This page shows an example of Granjon's 'couché' style of italic type. It is of the large *gros-romain* size (*c.* 16.5pt) and is used for the Prefaces of Jean Cousin's book. Interestingly, the printer Jean le Royer chose a roman type by Garamont (and not Granjon) for the main text of the book, the same one used by Michel de Vascosan *(C3)*. Note the extraordinary verve and style Granjon has given to this typeface. He provides many alternate letters, especially swash capitals, and two lively ampersands. Note also the heavier middle cross-strokes of **E** and **F**, and also the **K** and **R** with serifless tail.

PETIT CANON.

S'ils difent, Vien auec nous, tendons des embufches pour tuer: aguettons fecretement l'innocent encores qu'il ne nous ait point fait le pourquoy. Engloutiffons-les comme vn fepulcre, tous vifs, & tous entiers cōme ceux q̃ defcendent en la foffe. Nous trouuerons toute precieufe cheuance, nous remplirons nos maifons de butin.

ITALIQVE PETIT CANON.

Tu y auras ton lot parmi nous, il n'y aura qu'vne bourfe pour nous tous. Mon fils, ne te mets point en chemin auec eux: retire ton pied de leur fentier. Car leurs pieds courent au mal, & fe haftent pour refpandre le fang.

Baroque Types   *Jean Jannon   D1*

> dons des embufches pou
> aguettons fecretement l'ir
> encores qu'il ne nous ait p
> le pourquoy. Engloutif
> comme vn fepulcre, tous

Paris, Bibliothèque Mazarine, A. 15226(2). Jean Jannon, *Espreuves des caractères*. Printed in Sedan, France in 1621.

The page size is 9" x 6⅜" (229 x 164 mm). The text measure is 4⅛" (105 mm). The book has 20 unnumbered pages. The whole-page reproduction and the enlargement (two and a quarter times actual size) are both from the *Petit-canon* page.

Jean Jannon, born in Switzerland in 1580, later moved to Paris and, for a while, worked for the 'Stephanus' Press under Robert Estienne *(C2)*. Before 1607 he established his own printing press in that city. Harassed because of his Calvinist beliefs, Jannon moved to Sedan in 1611 as printer to 'his Excellency and the Sedanese Academy'. Having difficulty obtaining types from Paris, from 1615 onwards he began cutting and casting his own.

The Imprimerie royale was established in the Louvre in November 1640 under the patronage of Cardinal Richelieu. Six founts of Jannon's types were bought for the Imprimerie by the director, Sébastien Cramoisy, in March 1641 – the roman and italic matrices for three sizes: *gros-canon* (*c.* 36pt), *petit-canon* (*c.* 28pt), and *gros-parangon* (*c.* 22pt). The discovery of a contract for this purchase was first noted in a 1951 exhibition catalogue, repudiating the fanciful notion of Paul Beaujon (Beatrice Warde), made in 1927, that the types had been 'stolen' from Jannon by Richelieu's armies in Sedan.

Astonishingly, as James Mosley has discovered, only the two smaller sizes of italic types of Jannon, and *none* of his three romans were ever used by the Imprimerie royale during the 17th century. Eventually, his types were published in an 1845 specimen of the Imprimerie nationale, and (for the first time publicly) given the label *Caractères de l'Université* yet in fact attributing them to Claude Garamont! It was Jean Paillard who, in 1914, first raised doubts about this attribution to Garamont. Then in 1926 Beatrice Warde, who had compared the *Université* types with this 1621 specimen, identified them as those of Jean Jannon. But this startling revelation was too late to prevent many modern foundries from copying the *Caractères de l'Université* types and naming them 'Garamond' (see *C3*).

In order to show an early, authentic example of Jannon's roman types (the ones later called *Caractères de l'Université*), which were bought but not *used* by the Imprimerie royale in the 17th century, it has been necessary to go back to Jannon's own *Espreuves des caractères* published in 1621. His was the very first French type specimen book.

Jannon's *petit-canon* (*c.* 28pt) is fairly lightweight and sharply cut. Note the wide capital **E**; the tilted axis on **b**, **d**, **p**, and **q** (but not **o**); the bottom-heavy **e** with a high crossbar; and the narrow **s** and **v**. The top serifs on **i**, **m**, and **n** are very steeply angled and 'cupped'.

> en la foffe. Nous trouueroi

49

ral de leur ordre, & de bon nombre de docteurs Iesuistes, ont esté par arrest de la cour bruslez en public par l'executeur de la iustice. Que si vostre Maiesté veut s'en enquerir, elle trouuera qu'au college des Iesuistes de la Flesche, fondé par la liberalité du roy vostre pere de tres-glorieuse memoire, en la salle-basse du logis des peres y a vn grand tableau où sont representez les martyrs de l'ordre des Iesuistes, entre lesquels il y en a qui ont souffert le dernier supplice pour auoir entrepris sur la vie de leurs roys, & que cette punition y est appellée martyre ; & cela mis en veuë d'vne multitude de ieunesse, pour l'induire par ces exemples à paruenir à la gloire du martyre par le mesme chemin. Toutesfois ceux-là mesmes sans s'estre retractez, & sans auoir fait aucune declaration publique de condamner tels liures & telle doctrine, ont auiourd'huy l'oreille de nos roys, fouillent les secrets de leur conscience, & approchent le plus pres de leur personne.

RESPONSE.

La bonté de Dieu est si grande, qu'il conuertit d'ordinaire en bien le mal

Baroque Types   *Jean Jannon*   D2

Chicago, The Newberry Library, WING ZP 639 .P208. Cardinal duc de Richelieu, *Les principaux poincts de la foy catholique*. Printed in Paris, France by the Imprimerie Royale in 1642.

The page size is 14⅞" x 10½" (378 x 268 mm). The text measure is 5⅛" (130 mm). The book has 310 pages. The whole-page reproduction and the enlargement (two and a half times actual size) are taken from page 225.

Jean Jannon worked as a printer in Sedan for 33 years. In 1644 he accepted an invitation to join a learned Calvinist publisher and printer in Caen. When this clandestine operation was discovered and disbanded, he returned to Sedan and worked there until his death in 1658.

In Paris, Cardinal Richelieu convinced Louis XIII to set up a royal press for the express purpose of 'protecting the (Catholic) interests of State and Church' and, in November 1640, this Imprimerie royale was established in the Louvre. Just two years later it printed the book shown here, Richelieu's own defence of the Catholic faith against Protestant reformers, like Luther and Calvin.

Les principaux poincts is a very impressive volume. It is a large book with generous margins and cleanly printed type. Updike illustrated its roman and italic in his *Printing Types* of 1922 but, following the consensus of the time, he identified them as the types of 'Garamond'. Then Beatrice Warde, in her Introduction to the facsimile of Jannon's *Espreuves des caractères* (which she published in 1927), made reference to the Richelieu book, clearly stating that it was 'printed in Jannon's types'. So Updike, in his second edition of 1937, changed his attribution to 'Jannon'. Unfortunately, they were both (partially) wrong! The italic used in the Richelieu book is certainly Jannon's, and not Garamont's, but the roman used is actually one cut by Granjon. None of Jannon's romans, bought by the Imprimerie royale in 1641, were ever used in the 17th century (see *D1* notes).

The size of this italic type is Jannon's *petit-canon* (c. 28pt). The letterforms are sharply cut and the contrast between thick and thin strokes is distinctly marked. The sloping capitals may be a little heavy for the delicate lowercase. The slope of the lowercase is rather inconsistent (compare the almost upright **z** with the **p** and exaggerated slope of **m**); and **v** and **x** seem rather wide, but all these features give the letters a great deal of liveliness and character. Note the very distinctive capital **Q**, with its long, looped tail; the backward-leaning *&*, and the oversized, flamboyant lowercase **z**. Note also the cursive ligature for **is** (lines 8, 12, and 14 opposite).

ACTUS V. SCENA VI.

Demipho, Phormio, Chremes.

Diis magnas merito gratias habeo, atque ago,
Quando evenere hæc nobis, frater, prospere.
Quantum potest, nunc conveniendus Phormio est,
Priusquam dilapidet nostras triginta minas,
Ut auferamus. p. Demiphonem, si domi est, 5
Visam: ut quod— d. at nos ad te ibamus, Phormio.
p. De eadem hac fortasse causa. d. ita hercle. p. credidi.
Quid ad me ibatis? ridiculum: an veremini,
Ne non id facerem, quod recepissem semel? 9
Heus, quanta quanta hæc mea paupertas est, tamen
Adhuc curavi unum hoc quidem, ut mî esset fides.
c. Estne ea ita, ut dixi, liberalis? d. oppido.
p. Itaque ad vos venio nunciatum, Demipho,
Paratum me esse: ubi voltis, uxorem date.
Nam omnes posthabui mihi res, ita uti par fuit, 15
Postquam, tantopere id vos velle, animum advorteram.

d. At

Baroque Types   *Christoffel van Dijck* D3

> unc novas qui fcribunt, n
> laboriofa eft, ad me currit
> s eft, ad alium defertur gr
> eft pura oratio. experimin
> mque partem ingenium qu

Chicago, The Newberry Library, WING ZP 745 .C14. Terence, *Comoediae.* Printed in Cambridge, England at the University Press in 1701.

The page size is 11¼" x 8⅝" (288 x 212 mm). The overall text measure is 5⅞" (150 mm). The book has 520 pages. The whole-page reproduction is from page 393, the enlargement (two and a half times actual size) from page 169.

Christoffel van Dijck was born about 1605 in Dexheim, near Oppenheim, in what was then the Palatinate (now Germany). His family had emigrated from the Netherlands in the 16th century, and his father served as minister to the Dutch Protestant congregation in Frankelthal. Van Dijck moved to Amsterdam sometime before 1640 and initially took an apprenticeship as a goldsmith. A few years later, his profession was recorded as 'typefounder'.

In 1647 van Dijck set up his own type foundry, employing three assistants with Hendrik Claesz as foreman. At first, he was not very successful, and he ran into financial difficulties. To avoid ceding his typefounding tools and materials and other possessions to his creditors he, apparently, hid them with his neighbours! From 1650, however, his work prospered, and he became the leading punchcutter in the Netherlands, also supplying type to other printers like the Cambridge University Press, who used it for this edition of Terence.

When van Dijck died in 1669, the type foundry was entrusted to his son, Abraham, but he only outlived his father by three years. Most of Christoffel's punches, matrices, and standing type were then auctioned and came into the possession of the Amsterdam printer, Daniel Elsevier.

This handsome volume from the University Press at Cambridge shows the *double pica* (*c.* 22pt) type of van Dijck to great advantage. The lines of text are widely spaced and cleanly printed. The capitals are generally quite wide, and many of them, like **A**, **E**, **H**, **N**, and **U**, have a strong thick/thin contrast. The lowercase has comparatively short ascenders, resulting in a large x-height. Overall, the axis on the rounded letters is horizontal (except for **c** and **e**). While most of the serifs of the lowercase are angled and bracketed (except the descenders), those on **u** are horizontal and hairline. Note the rather narrow **a**, like that of Kis (*D5*) – perhaps it is a 'Dutch' trait! Note also the sharply cut exits on **c** and **e**; the unevenly weighted lower bowl of **g**; the 'cupped' apex on capital **A**, and the long, elegant tail of **Q**.

> quanta hæc mea paupertas eft,

PHORMIONIS ARGUMENTUM,

C. SULPICIO APOLLINARI AUCTORE.

Chremetis frater aberat peregre Demipho,
Relicto Athenis Antiphone filio.
Chremes clam habebat Lemni uxorem & filiam,
Athenis aliam conjugem, & amantem unice
Gnatum fidicinam. mater e Lemno advenit 5
Athenas: moritur. virgo sola (aberat Chremes)
Funus procurat. ibi eam visam Antipho
Cum amaret, opera parasiti uxorem accipit.
Pater & Chremes reversi fremere. dein minas
Triginta dant parasito, ut illam conjugem 10
Haberet ipse: argento hoc emitur fidicina.
Uxorem retinet Antipho a patruo agnitam.

Baroque Types   *Christoffel van Dijck* D4

Chicago, The Newberry Library, WING ZP 745 .C14. Terence, *Comoediae*. Printed in Cambridge, England at the University Press in 1701.

The page size is 11¼" x 8⅝" (288 x 212 mm). The overall text measure is 5⅞" (150 mm). The book has 520 pages. The whole-page reproduction is from page 326, the enlargement (two and a half times actual size) from page 406.

The heading of the famous type specimen published in 1681 by the widow of the Amsterdam printer Daniel Elsevier suggests that all the types shown on that specimen were cut by Christoffel van Dijck. In fact, modern research has shown that only a few were by van Dijck; quite a number of them were actually 16th-century French types cut by Garamont, Granjon and others.

Nevertheless, van Dijck has a deservedly fine reputation. Warren Chappell considered him 'one of the greatest 17th-century punchcutters', and Stanley Morison, rather strangely, wrote, '(although) his typefaces are not as important to the historian as those of Garamond *(sic)*, they are certainly more beautiful'. But van Dijck's reputation is based on much less evidence than was once thought. Regrettably, very few authentic punches or matrices of van Dijck have survived. In the Enschedé Foundry collection in Haarlem, only those for one italic (a *klein text curcyf*) and three blackletter fonts are extant.

Most of what we know of Christoffel van Dijck's types is from other type specimens or printed books, like this well-designed Terence from the University of Cambridge Press, printed in 1701.

These pages, with van Dijck's *double pica* (*c.* 22pt) italic type, are introductions to the individual texts of Terence's *Comoediae*. Like the main text pages set in roman type (see D3), the lines of italic are generously spaced and cleanly printed. The same thick/thin contrast can be seen in the italic capitals as in van Dijck's roman. The sharply-cut italic lowercase letters have a very consistent slope, large x-height, and a strong cursive character (see **m**, **n**, and **u** and also the **f** and **ſ**). The serifs on the acsenders are all horizontal with minimal bracketing, while those on the descenders are hairline, like his roman. Note the lively form of **g** and exuberant **v**; the 'uncial' form of **h**; the unusual **p**; the almost detached bowl of **q**; and the wide **x**.

55

CXXXXI.
insieme ad argento finalmente si roppe, e lo squarcio principiato nell' argento della saldatura tirò innanzi per l' oro ancora.

Esperienze intorno agli agghiacciamenti.

ESPERIENZA

Per misurare quanta sia la forza della rarefazione dell' acqua serrata nell' agghiacciarsi.

PER arrivare a questa misura fu pensato di far fabbricare una palla di metallo come l' altre, ma tonda, e secondo il nostro giudizio tanto più grossa che la forza della rarefazione non giugnesse a romperla, e questa empierla d'acqua, serrarla colla sua vite, e metterla ad agghiacciare conforme al solito. Così dunque fu fatto, e da principio trovammo, che l'acqua vi s'agghiacciava senza trasudamento, e senza rottura apparente del metallo. Si rimesse pertanto la palla in sul torno, e proccurando di mantenerle il più che fosse possibile la similitudine della figura; se n'andò levando per tutto uniformemente, per dir così, una sottilissima sfoglia. Ciò fatto si rimesse nel ghiaccio con dell' altr' acqua per la seconda volta, e ne meno questa essendosi aperta, quantunque si fosse agghiacciata, si ritornò tante volte ad assottigliarla con insensibili detrazioni, finchè se le vedde fare un sottilissimo pelo. Questa medesima esperienza si replicò con tre palle, la più grossa delle quali era secondo il profilo segnato nella x. figura. Sicchè ci parve di poter dire esser quella la massima grossezza superata dalla rarefazione dell' acqua serrata nell' agghiacciarsi. Arrivatosi a questo ci venne voglia di ridur questa forza a quella d' un peso morto: ed il modo di conseguirlo ci pareva che fosse il far gettare della stessa pasta, e crudezza di metallo un' anello di grossezza uguale alla

Acqua serrata in una palla d'ottone grossissima s'agghiaccia senza trasudare dalla vite, e senza rottura manifesta del metallo.

Modo di vitricare la massima grossezza dell'ottone superabile dalla forza dell'acqua.

FIG. X.

Come si possa ridur tal forza a quella d'un peso morto.

Baroque Types *Miklós Tótfalusi Kis* D5

> che miglio. Sarà ancor
> to da noi fiano lontano
> da terra fi creino i tu
> fi vede il baleno a che
> remo poi la diftanza

University of Illinois at Urbana-Champaign Library, RBML IUQ00233. Accademia del cimento, *Saggi di naturali esperienze*. Printed in Florence, Italy by G F Cecchi in 1691.

The page size is 14⅞" x 9¾" (378 x 247 mm). The main text measure is 6" (152 mm). The book has 308 pages. The whole-page reproduction is taken from page 141, the enlargement (three times actual size) from page 245.

Miklós Tótfalusi Kis, or for simplicity 'Nicholas Kis' (pronounced 'Kish'), was born in Hungary in 1650. Following his theological education at the Transylvania Reformed Church College, he was approached by his Church leaders to edit a new Hungarian Bible and prepare it for printing in Holland by Daniel Elsevier. In response to this Kis moved to Amsterdam in 1680. He became deeply involved in the whole publication process and was actually apprenticed to a notable Dutch punchcutter (almost certainly, Dirck Voskens). Within three years he had decided to print the Bible himself, and he created his own types for the purpose!

While in Amsterdam he printed four books in Hungarian – 3,500 copies of the Bible, plus a Psalter, and 4,200 copies each of 'pocket' editions of the Psalter and New Testament. His Amsterdam type specimen (*c.* 1686), shows 32 series of roman and italics types, as well as greek and hebrew founts, and even tiny musical notation.

Nicholas Kis gained an international reputation, and he sold his types and matrices to printers in England, Sweden, Poland and other European countries. The Ehrhardt foundry in Leipzig published a broadside Specimen (*c.* 1720) which showed some of the types of Kis, simply calling them *Holländischen Schrifften*. In his autobiographical *Mentsége* of 1698, Kis recalls two representatives arriving in Amsterdam to purchase his types for a printer and typefounder in Tuscany. Confirmation of his story has been discovered by Berta Maracchi Biagiarelli in the State Archives in Florence, which she published in 1965. The documents reveal that indeed two envoys from the Florentine printing establishment of Giovanni Filippo Cecchi purchased matrices, and even *punches*, for 14 roman and italic types (also some greek and hebrew) from the punchcutter 'Niccolò Chis' in Amsterdam.

In this splendid book printed in 1691, we can see some of those types of Kis sensitively used by Cecchi. The text was set in his *parangon* (*c.* 20pt) roman and italic.

The typefaces of Kis have a distinctive style. In the lowercase letters, note the large x-height, narrow forms, and the definite contrast of stroke. Note also the very narrow **a**; the bottom-heavy **c** and **e**; the tilted axis on **b**, **d**, **p**, and **q**, yet the horizontal (almost backward) axis on the **o**. All the serifs are angled and bracketed, except for **u**, but the descenders have flat, hairline serifs. Also note the ligatures fi, fi, ff, and ft. Capital **Q** is heavy and has a long tail.

> on infenfibili detrazioni, finchè

INDICE

Canne di vetro come si debbano fare, acciò si possano agevolmente chiudere colle dita. pag. 50.

Carta bianca esposta al riverbero d'un grande specchio ardente s'accende. pag. 266.

Cerchi dell'acqua più veloci secondo la varia forza, che gli produce. pag. 243.

Ciambella di Cristallo, vedi Cristallo

Ciò che fa varietà nell'attrazione dell'ambra, lo fa in tutti i corpi elettrici. pag. 218.

Corpi pregni maggiormente di luce. pag. 266.

Cristallo si distende dall'acqua calda, e si ritira dalla fredda. pag. 186.

D

DIAMANTE come s'ingeneri secondo Platone 128. *Chiamato ramo dell'oro dal medesimo.* pag. 128.

Diamanti in tavola tirano meno di quelli gruppiti. pag. 231.

Digestione di alcuni animali, come si faccia. pag. 268.

Esperienze varie intorno a ciò. ivi.

E

EFFETTO mirabile del calore in sublimare un liquore rinchiuso. pag. 258.

Esperienze, che richieggono misura esatta del tempo. pag. 16.

Esperienza del Gassendo d'attaccare il ghiaccio a una tavola spruzzandolo di sale verissima. pag. 174.

Esperienze in qualunque modo utili nell'esame delle cose naturali. pag. 197.

Estrusione de' corpi nota agli antichi. pag. 207.

Insegnata apertamente da Platone nel Timeo. pag. 208.

Estrusione del fuoco, e dell'umido fatta dall'aria secondo i sentimenti di Platone. pag. 208.

Ciò

Baroque Types   *Miklós Tótfalusi Kis*   D6

University of Illinois at Urbana-Champaign Library, RBML IUQ00233. Accademia del cimento, *Saggi di naturali esperienze*. Printed in Florence, Italy by G F Cecchi in 1691.

The page size is 14⅞" x 9¾" (378 x 247 mm). The text measure is 6" (152 mm). The book has 308 pages. The whole-page reproduction is taken from page 279, the enlargement (three times actual size) from page 52.

Nicholas Kis returned to Hungary in 1689 and set up a printing establishment in Kolozsvár. Before he died in 1702 he published more than 100 titles there – textbooks on law, ethics, and history – editing, typesetting, and printing each one himself! Two autobiographical works, the *Apologia Bibliorum* of 1697 and his *Mentsége* of 1698, not only reveal much about his own life, but also give important insights into the world of 17th-century printing and publishing.

Until quite recently, the types of Kis have unfortunately been attributed to the Dutch punchcutter Anton Janson. Two early German type specimens (Ehrhardt *c.* 1720 and Drugulin in 1874) showed the typefaces of Kis without crediting him, simply calling them *Holländischen Schrifften*, 'Dutch letters'. But in the 1924 specimen of D Stempel in Frankfurt those same types were labelled '*Janson Antiqua und Kursiv*'. It was not until 1954 that Harry Carter and George Buday first identified Kis as the originator of these types *(Linotype Matrix,* 18). The 1686 Amsterdam specimen (the only-known copy is now in the National Hungarian Museum in Budapest) has a colophon naming 'Nikolaas Kis' as the punchcutter, and this has provided the vital clue as to the true creator of the 'Janson' types of Stempel.

Since the 'rediscovery' of Kis, knowledge of him has been widely extended by the researches of József Molnár, György Haiman, and others. A major biography of Nicholas Kis by Haiman was published in 1972 in Budapest, and a very useful English translation was made available in 1983.

This large scientific book, printed by G F Cecchi in 1691, is a remarkable work, profusely illustrated with over 70 engraved diagrams, each one occupying a whole page. It includes a full Index, printed throughout in the *parangon* (*c.* 20pt) italics of Kis. These are lively and full of cursive character, and nicely complement his roman face *(D5)*.

Overall, the letters have a consistent slope and are quite narrow; see **b**, **g**, and especially **o**. Note the very low branching on **m**, **n**, **r**, **u**, and even on the 'uncial' **h**; the flourished **v** and **z** (the latter is noticeably upright); and the bracketed ascenders and the hairline serifs on the descenders, just like his roman lowercase. There are many ligatures: ff, fi, fl, fi, ff, ft, also fs and ſt. Perhaps the most distinctive earmark of Kis' italic is the angled entrance stroke on **m**, **n**, and **r**.

JUVENALIS

SATIRA IV.

Ecce iterum Crispinus, et est mihi sæpe vocandus
Ad partes, monstrum nulla virtute redemtum
A vitiis, æger, solaque libidine fortis:
Delicias viduæ tantum spernatur adulter.
Quid refert igitur, quantis jumenta fatiget   5
Porticibus? quanta nemorum vectetur in umbra?
Jugera quot vicina foro, quas emerit ædes?
Nemo malus felix; minime corruptor, et idem
Incestus, cum quo nuper vittata jacebat
Sanguine adhuc vivo terram subitura sacerdos.   10
Sed nunc de factis levioribus: et tamen alter
Si fecisset idem, caderet sub judice morum.
Nam quod turpe bonis, Titio Seioque, decebat
Crispinum. Quid agas, quum dira et fœdior omni
Crimine persona est? Mullum sex millibus emit,   15
Æquantem sane paribus sestertia libris,
Ut perhibent, qui de magnis majora loquuntur.
Consilium laudo artificis, si munere tanto
Præcipuam in tabulis ceram senis abstulit orbi.
Est ratio ulterior, magnæ si misit amicæ,   20

Baroque Types   *William Caslon I* D7

>ebetur magnus patinæ fu
rgillam atque rotam citi
empore jam, Cæfar, figu
icit digna viro fententia.
uxuriam imperii veteren

Chicago, The Newberry Library, WING ZP 845 .C4375. Juvenal, *Satirae*. Printed in London, England by Charles Whittingham at the Chiswick Press in 1845.

The page size is 10⅞" x 8⅝" (275 x 220 mm). The overall text measure is 4¾" (119 mm). The book has 99 folios. The whole-page reproduction is taken from folio E ii(v), the enlargement (three and a half times actual size) from folio F i(R).

William Caslon was born in 'Hales Owen', then situated in Shropshire; his baptism was registered on 23 April 1693. In his early teens he was apprenticed to a London gun engraver. (Recently, a ship's musketoon, dated 1715, was discovered in the Tower of London, its lock stamped with the name 'CASLON'.) He also learned about the 'chasing' of silver plate, and the cutting of tooling letters for bookbinders.

Encouraged by the printers William Bowyer and Samuel Palmer, Caslon established a London type foundry in 1720. After his first type (probably the hebrew fount 'without points' cut for Bowyer), he was commissioned by the Society for Promoting Christian Knowledge to make an arabic type. Samuel Palmer used this type for a Psalter in 1725 and, two years later, a New Testament. The story goes that Caslon included his name, set in a *pica* (c. 12pt) roman type, on an arabic sheet and Palmer, noticing it, suggested that he cut the complete fount. This type, Caslon's first roman, was used by Bowyer for the end notes of a book printed in 1725.

By 1730 Caslon 'had eclipsed most of his competitors' (William Ged, *Memoirs)*. His type was of such high quality that it ended, once and for all, English dependence on the importation of Dutch type. The famous 1734 Caslon type specimen contains a full range of types: 14 sizes each of roman and italic, two blackletter, three hebrew, four greek, and six other non-Latin founts.

James Mosley praises Caslon's *great primer* (c. 18pt) type as a 'magnificent achievement'. Although Caslon partly based it on Dutch type (used by his friend William Bowyer, and seen in specimens of Voskens c. 1695, and Adamsz and Ente c. 1700) it is, nevertheless, a fine independent typeface.

A century later, in 1839, Charles Whittingham took over the management of the Chiswick Press from his uncle. He found some cases of old Caslon type and, probably at the suggestion of William Pickering his publisher, he used it on five title pages printed that year. Whittingham also decided to use Caslon types, newly-cast, for special imprints in 1844 and 1845. One of them, the beautifully-printed Juvenal shown here, printed on toned paper, displays Caslon's *great primer* type at its best.

The lowercase letters have a consistent medium weight, good baseline alignment, and very few idiosyncratic features. Characteristic capitals include **A** with 'cupped' apex; **C** with double serifs; a long, heavy tail on **Q**; a straight-legged **R**; and **T** with outward-sloping serifs on the cross stroke.

Quid refert igitur, quantis jumenta fati

61

From the Diary of

1635.

little one, be a Crown of rejoycing to thee as thou art to me; lead him early to *God*, my Daughter; to the *God* who has given him unto thee.   Deare *Mother!*

August 4, Tuesday.

Early in the fore-noon my honoured and deare *Mother* took her Departure: Let me think more of meeting againe than of the present payne of Parting. Some lines of *Ben Jonson* I do remember are fwetely written to this effecte, they were given me by a young Friend at parting, who I beleeve was lefs indifferent towardes me, than I to him:

That Love's a bitter fweet I ne'er conceive
Till the fower Minute comes of taking leave,
And then I tafte it: But as Men drinke up
In haft the bottom of a medicin'd Cup,
And take fome firrup after, foe do I
To put all relifh from my Memorie
Of parting, drowne it in the hope to meet
Shortly againe; and make our Abfence fweet.
Beloved

Baroque Types   *William Caslon I D8*

> *keepe them in the Path of*
> *them in Danger, comfor*
> *when they come to paſſe t*
> *Shadow of Death, let their*
> *be afraid: but let them*

Chicago, The Newberry Library, Wing zp 845 .w613. Hannah Mary Rathbone, *The Diary of Lady Willoughby*. Printed in London, England by Charles Whittingham at the Chiswick Press in 1844.

The page size is 8⅜" x 6⅝" (212 x 167 mm). The text measure is 4" (102 mm). The book has 176 pages. The whole-page reproduction is taken from page 16, the enlargement (three and a half times actual size) from page 68.

William Caslon (1693–1766) began making type in 1720. His son, William II (1720–1778), also a punchcutter, became a partner in the family firm, maybe from as early as 1738 – he certainly contributed 11 new founts to the specimen of 1742. When *his* son, William III (1754–1833), sold his share of the business in 1792, Elizabeth, widow of William II, took over the management, and the firm flourished for a while as 'H W Caslon' until 1937 when it was eventually acquired by the Stephenson Blake foundry.

William Caslon I, however, set a very high standard for his descendents to follow. His *great primer* 'Italick', for example, is outstanding. Before being included on the 1734 type specimen, it was also shown on what was undoubtedly a proof sheet, *c.* 1730, the unique copy of which is now in the British Library. Most likely Caslon modelled his italic on a Dutch type (used in a book printed in 1726 by his friend William Bowyer), but he did so in his own original style.

Contrary to the overwhelming typographic preference for 'Bodoni-like' types, during most of the 19th century, Charles Whittingham decided to revive the use of Caslon's 18th-century type for special imprints of his Chiswick Press. The first book he printed, using newly cast Caslon type, was *The Diary of Lady Willoughby*. This marvellously well-printed book shows Caslon's *great primer* (*c.* 18pt) types at their finest. *The Diary*, a fictitious account of aristocratic domestic life during the tumultuous English Civil War (1642–1648), was published by Longmans in April 1844. Whittingham deliberately gave the book a 17th-century 'look' with ruled borders and decorative headings, retaining the old spelling, even long **s** (ſ). The use of Caslon's *Great Primer* types added to the 'antique' effect.

In *The Diary* italic was used as a complementary face to its roman text. Some of the sloped capitals, like Caslon's roman ones *(D7)*, are maybe a little too heavy. Note the flat top on **A** and its excessive slant, and the cursive nature of capital **J**. Characteristic lowercase letters include 'uncial' **h** and cursive **v** and **w**. Numerous ligatures are used; note **fh**, **ff**, and **ft** in the illustrations. The lowercase **r** seems to be poorly spaced. See the word 'afraid' (above), and the word 'sirrup' (opposite). This defect also seen in the *great primer* 'Italick' of Caslon's early type specimens.

To put all reliſh from my Memorie

63

Text Romein.
Fr. *Gros Romein gros œil.*
Engl. Great Primer Roman.
Hoogd. *Tertia Antiqua.*

Lors qu'Aspasie étoit concubine d'Artaxerxès : On ne sauroit lui donner moins de vingt ans à la mort de Cyrus : elle avoit donc soixante - quinze ans lors qu'un nouveau Roi la demande comme une grace particuliere. PLTGA
ABCDEFHIJKMNOQSU
VWXYZÆ ÆABCDEFGHIJKL
MMNOPQRSTUVWYZ ÇĒŐŸŖ
1234567890†()[¶§!?áòıŭmñ

J. M. Fleischman sculpsit. 1739.

Text Curcyf.
Fr. *Gros Romain gros œil Italique.*
Engl. Great Primer Cursiv.
Hoogd. *Tertia Cursiv.*

Ciceron menagea toûjours Dolabella le plus doucement qu'il put. Il avoit sans doute plus d'habileté que de fermeté, & il voioit que le parti de Pompée se ruïnoit de plus en plus par les contiuelles victoires de Jules
ABCDEFGHIKLMNO
PQRSTVWXYZ. UJÆ

J. M. Fleischman sculpsit. 1739.

Neoclassical Types　　　　　　　　　　　　　　　　　　　　　*Johann Fleischman* E2

> foixante - quinze ans
> nouveau Roi la dema
> une grace particuliere
> ABCDEFHIJKMNO
> devint si fort amoureux
> oit belle nonobstånt l'âge

Chicago, The Newberry Library, CASE WING z 40546 .2642. Johann Enschedé, *Proef van Letteren.* Printed in Haarlem, in the Netherlands in 1768.

The page size is 8¾" x 5¼" (221 x 132 mm). The text measure is 2⅝" (68 mm). The book has 105 unnumbered folios. The whole-page reproduction is of the *text romein* and *text curcyf* page, and the enlargements (three and a half times actual size) are from the same page (for the roman lowercase), and the *text curcyf op paragon* page (for the italic).

Joan (Johann) Michael Fleischman, born near Nuremberg, Germany in 1707, was trained as a punchcutter, quickly becoming very skilful. He was employed for a short time at the Luther foundry in Frankfurt before moving to Holland in 1728. He found work there with the publishers Alberts and Uytwerf, first in The Hague and then later in Amsterdam. Fleischman left them in 1732 in order to set up a punchcutting business on his own. His reputation gained him a contract with one of Haarlem's major printing and typefounding companies, that of Izaak and Johann Enschedé. Although Fleischman later produced type for other foundries, his congenial partnership with the Enschedés lasted from 1743 until his death in 1768 and resulted in almost 100 fonts for them – widely varied romans, italics, blackletter, greeks, arabics, armenians, and even musical notation.

Fleischman's brilliant engraving skill was legendary, even in his own day. His *diamant* (*c.* 4pt) roman and blackletter was 'the smallest type to be found in all Europe'. Charles Enschedé, director of the foundry from 1887, considered Fleischman 'the greatest punchcutter that ever lived and that will probably ever live'!

The Fleischman types shown here, cut in 1739, are from the Enschedé specimen of 1768, issued just a few months after his death. The *text romein* and *text curcyf* are equivalent in size to the English *great primer* (*c.* 18pt). His letterforms have a lot of individuality and personality – note the 'forked' serifs on capitals **E**, **F**, **L**, **T**, and **Z**, and the 'cupped' serifs on some of the lowercase ascenders. Perhaps Fleischman was the first type designer to add a *whimsical* quality to roman text type. His portrait (see *Frontispiece*, page 2) shows him to be an affable soul, maybe even a little mischievous!

Overall, his letterforms have a large x-height, strongly contrasted thick and thin strokes, often with a horizontal axis and hairline serifs. The curved strokes of capital **O**, and some others, are rather abrupt. These features somewhat anticipate the later types of Didot and Bodoni (see *F1* and *F2*).

> lui donner moins de vingt ans à la

67

PETIT-PARANGON.

Les Tyrans sont les premiers esclaves de la tyrannie, & ne sont pas les moins malheureux Julien l'Apostat dit judicieusement qu'il n'y a que les tyrans qui donnent leurs succès pour des raisons, & leurs caprices pour loix.

Neoclassical Types *Pierre-Simon Fournier* E3

> ont chacun un ton
> de voix, des geſtes
> & des mines qui
> leur font propres.
> Ce rapport, bon ou

Chicago, The Newberry Library, CASE WING Z 40539 .311. Pierre-Simon Fournier, *Les Caractères de l'Imprimerie.* Printed in Paris, France in 1764.

The page size is 7⅛" x 4⅞" (181 x 125 mm). The text measure is 1⅞" (49 mm). The book has 132 pages. The whole-page reproduction is taken from page 62, the enlargement (three and a half times actual size) from page 64.

Pierre-Simon was the most distinguished of the remarkable Fournier family of type founders. His father Jean-Claude managed the long-estabished Le Bé foundry in Paris from 1698 until he died in 1729. His brother, Jean-Pierre – often referred to as *l'aîné* (the elder), actually bought the foundry one year later. In all, four generations of Fourniers were involved either in the manufacture or use of printing types.

Born in Auxerre in 1712, Pierre-Simon – who called himself Fournier *le jeune* (the younger), returned to Paris at the age of 17, and for a short time he worked with his father at the Le Bé foundry. By 1736 he had branched out on his own and began by engraving printers' ornaments in wood, and making large punches for 'poster' types cast in metal.

In his short lifetime (he died aged 56) he was acclaimed as the pre-eminent type designer of his day, yet he was also an energetic scholar-printer. Fournier not only wrote extensively on the history and practice of printing, but he was also an inventor who made numerous improvements to the techniques of punchcutting and casting type.

In addition, Pierre-Simon produced four excellent specimen books displaying his finely-cut types, some with an immense range of size, from *c.* 5pt to *c.* 108pt. Two of them appeared as early as 1742 – the *Modéles des Caractères de l'Imprimerie* (a quarto volume in landscape format), and a pocket-sized edition, *Caractères de l'Imprimerie.* The third specimen, *Les Caractères de l'Imprimerie,* was printed in 1764. The sharply printed *petit-parangon* (*c.* 20pt) types shown here, are from that edition. Volume II of his huge *Manuel Typographique*, published just before he died in 1768, was also an annotated specimen of types.

Fournier's roman face is often considered to be the first 'Transitional' type – retaining aspects of earlier styles, but incorporating new design ideas. The angled serifs at the midline and on the ascenders, and the tilted axes on **c** and **e**, are reminiscent of the older styles of Aldus and Garamont. But the slight increase in thick/thin contrast, the common height for ascenders and capitals, and the flat serifs on **u** and **d**, all anticipate the later types of Didot and Bodoni. Note the 'energetic' lower bowl of the **g** and the flat bottom on **t**. Maybe lowercase **y** is a shade too wide, and **x** a little narrow.

judicieuſement tyransqui donne

PETIT-PARANGON.

Le grand usage du monde & la connoissance de ce qui s'y passe, tiennent lieu souvent de talens, d'esprit, de mérite, & même de vertus; mais lorsqu'il faut compter avec soi-même, c'est toute autre chose.

Neoclassical Types *Pierre-Simon Fournier* E4

beaucoup de gens ont de la reconnoiſ-ſance pour les mé-diocres ; mais il n'y a quaſi perſonne qui

Chicago, The Newberry Library, CASE WING Z 40539 .311. Pierre-Simon Fournier, *Les Caractères de l'Imprimerie*. Printed in Paris, France in 1764.

The page size is 7⅛" x 4⅞" (181 x 125 mm). The text measure is 1⅞" (48 mm). The book has 132 pages. The whole-page reproduction is taken from page 63, the enlargement (three and a half times actual size) is from page 65, and shows the same type cast on a larger body.

Although Pierre-Simon Fournier was an extremely skilful punchcutter and typefounder, he devoted a great deal of his time and energy to researching and writing about the history of typography and the technical aspects of printing. These topics are discussed at length in his *Avis* (Introduction) to the *Modéles des Caractères de l'Imprimerie* of 1742.

Fournier was at ease among the scientists, artists, and craftsmen of Paris and contributed enthusiastically to learned journals and to Diderot's monumental *Encyclopédie*. His 1764 *Manuel Typographique* (Vol. I) was the very first French publication to describe in detail the intricate techniques of punchcutting, matrix making, and typefounding. In the days when the sizing of type was inconsistent, Pierre-Simon also developed his own point system claiming that he was the first to rationalise the existing confusion. However, he failed to acknowledge the earlier, more precise system devised by Sébastien Truchet for the *romains du roi* (see *Introduction*). The final version of Fournier's 'Table of proportions' was included in Volume I of his *Manuel* published in 1764.

Fournier's italic types are often praised for their originality and novel style. They are distinct from his roman face but in harmony with it. He himself admitted that he intended to reform the italics of former times 'by bringing them a little closer to our style of writing'.

The examples shown here are Fournier's *petit-parangon* italics (*c.* 20pt). They reveal something of the 'novelty' of his designs. Compared with the *'cancellaresca'* italics of Griffo and Arrighi *(B5* and *B6)*, they do seem to resemble a rather 'sloped roman' style of letter. While his italic forms have a definite slant, they are more formal in character than other italic types. Their ascenders and descenders are fairly short, the arch shapes are wide and quite rounded, and all the midline serifs are bracketed and flat. Harry Carter, however, considered them 'the most legible of all italics'.

Note the flowing, cursive quality of **f** and long **s** (**ſ**). In some larger sizes of Pierre-Simon's italics, lowercase **a** and **d** are peculiar. It seems as though a letter **c** has gate-crashed! See his *double-canon* (*c.* 56pt) letters, inset above.

qu'il faut compter *e autre choſe*

71

Quam maxume servire vostris commodis;
Exemplum statuite in me, ut adolescentuli
Vobis placere studeant potius, quam sibi.

ACTUS I. SCENA I.

CHREMES, MENEDEMUS.

Quanquam hæc inter nos nuper notitia admodum est,
Inde adeo quod agrum in proximo hic mercatus es,
Nec rei fere sane amplius quidquam fuit:
Tamen vel virtus tua me, vel vicinitas,

Neoclassical Types *John Baskerville E5*

Chicago, The Newberry Library, WING ZP 745 .B30646. Terence, *Comoediae.* Printed by John Baskerville in Birmingham, England in 1772.

The page size is 11¼" x 9⅛" (285 x 231 mm). The overall text measure is 5⅛" (130 mm). The book has 364 pages. The whole-page reproduction is taken from page 131, the enlargement (three and a half times actual size) from page 3.

Although John Baskerville did not begin experimenting with printing until he was about 44 years old, the quality of his presswork and type design is astonishing, and his impact on typography, especially in France and Italy, was enormous. He was an amateur, self-taught printer, but he spared neither time nor money in his pursuit of perfection.

Baskerville fully involved himself in every aspect of the printing process. His type designs were innovative (lighter and more sharply cut than ever before) and, seeking the best way to print them, he made meticulous improvements to the paper, ink, and even his printing press. He was the first to use smooth 'wove' paper, and the first to 'hot-press' his printed sheets. He developed his own blacker and faster-drying ink. He turned his printing press into a precision instrument, painstakingly grinding the platen and stone perfectly flat and smooth until he could claim, 'if you rest one end of the plate on the stone, & let the other fall the height of an inch; it falls soft as if you dropt it on feathers…' (All quotations in *E5* and *E6* are from original sources, recorded by Pardoe, with 18th-century spelling retained.)

To ensure the sharpest impression, he never re-used his types. 'It was Mr Baskervills custom to melt the Types when they had completed One Book so that he always printed with new Letter.' And he was meticulous in printing, even matching the lines of text on both sides of the sheet. 'My Printing is, and always has been strictly in Register, one line falling on the Back of the other, which preserves the Colour and Beauty of the Whole.'

This Terence of 1772, completed just three years before he died, exhibits his dramatic, undecorated page layout: large margins, wide interlinear spaces, and letterspaced capitals – all enhancing his elegant *great primer* (*c.* 18pt) roman type.

Baskerville's letterforms are original. He claimed 'my Letters are not (one of them) copied from any other; but are wrought from my own Ideas only'. The types of Baskerville quintessentially define what was once known as the 'Transitional' style – lightweight letters with fine thin strokes, very slight axis to the curved forms, angled serifs on the ascenders, and more open counters. Note his splendid capital **Q**, (see also the back cover of *Historical Types)*, the earmark lowercase **g** (its lower bowl unjoined), and ligatures ct, ft.

73

ANDRIÆ ARGUMENTUM,

C. SULPICIO APOLLINARI AUCTORE.

Sororem falso creditam meretriculæ,
Genere Andriæ, Glycerium vitiat Pamphilus:
Gravidaque facta, dat fidem, uxorem sibi
Fore hanc: nam aliam pater ei desponderat
Gnatam Chremetis: atque ut amorem comperit,
Simulat futuras nuptias; cupiens, suus
Quid haberet animi filius, cognoscere.
Davi suasu non repugnat Pamphilus.
Sed ex Glycerio natum ut vidit puerulum
Chremes, recusat nuptias, generum abdicat:
Mox filiam Glycerium insperato agnitam
Dat Pamphilo hanc, aliam Charino conjugem.

P.

Neoclassical Types   *John Baskerville E6*

> imique sese angebat, facti
> x ut revorsus est, clam pc
> Clitiphonem. Is amabat
> m arcesseret cupitam Anti
> ejus Bacchis venit amica

Chicago, The Newberry Library, Wing zp 745 .b30646. Terence, *Comoediae*. Printed by John Baskerville in Birmingham, England in 1772.

    The page size is 11¼" x 9⅛" (285 x 231 mm). The overall text measure is 5⅛" (130 mm). The book has 364 pages. The whole-page reproduction is taken from page 2, the enlargement (three times actual size) from page 128.

John Baskerville was baptised in Wolverly Parish Church near Kidderminster on 28 January 1706 (actually 1707 according to our modern calendar). We know little of his youth, but he said of himself that he was 'an early admirer of the beauty of Letters' and he was 'desirous of contributing to the perfection of them'. We can recognise this ambition in a carved slate 'advertisement' (*c.* 1728) announcing in elaborately flourished letters, 'Grave Stones, Cut in any of the Hands, By John Baskervill, Writing Master'.

    In 1742 Baskerville submitted a patent for the process of 'japanning' (a method of decorating and varnishing metal articles such as picture frames and cabinets). Clearly this provided him with a considerable fortune; just six years later he was able to move to a seven-acre estate near Birmingham called 'Easy Hill', and he spent substantial sums of money building a large house, workshops, stables, and garden.

    This wealth enabled Baskerville to embark on his printing endeavours. Printing and publishing, however, turned out to be a very expensive 'hobby', so he never totally abandoned japanning. A letter dated 20 July 1773, just two years before he died, reveals him still trading in japanned ware.

    Baskerville fully involved himself in every aspect of the printing process but, although he designed the letters for his types, the punches were almost certainly cut for him by John Handy. A 1792 magazine records the death of 'Mr John Handy, the artist who cut the punches for Baskerville's types'. A note written for Sarah, Baskerville's widow, mentions a 'very honest man' (presumably John Handy) 'which performed all the manual opperations… of fileing the punchions, making the letter moulds & every other improvement which Mr Baskervill made in printing'.

    Baskerville's elegant italic type, shown here in *great primer* size (*c.* 18pt) has many of the features of cursive penmanship to be expected of a 'Writing Master'. Note the consistent forward slope for all letters, capitals and lowercase; looped entrance and exit strokes on **i**, **j**, **m**, **n**, **r**, **u**, **x**, and **y**; cursive forms of **f**, **j**, **v**, and long **s** (**ſ**). Capital **Q** and lowercase **g** are earmarks for Baskerville italics, as well as for his roman letters (see *E5*). The hairline entrance stroke on lowercase **p** betrays a quirk of his own handwriting. The italic capitals are perhaps a little tall and rather heavy.

> *ex Glycerio natum ut vidit pueru*

AENEIDOS
LIBER IV.

At regina, gravi jam dudum saucia cura,
Vulnus alit venis, et cæco carpitur igni.
Multa viri virtus animo, multusque recursat
Gentis honos: hærent infixi pectore vultus,
Verbaque; nec placidam membris dat cura quietem.
Postera Phœbea lustrabat lampade terras,
Humentemque aurora polo dimoverat umbram;
Cum sic unanimam alloquitur male sana sororem:
   Anna soror, quæ me suspensam insomnia terrent!
Quis novus hic nostris successit sedibus hospes!
Quem sese ore ferens! quam forti pectore, et armis!
Credo equidem, nec vana fides, genus esse Deorum.
Degeneres animos timor arguit. Heu! quibus ille
Jactatus fatis! quæ bella exhausta canebat!
Si mihi non animo fixum immotumque sederet
Ne cui me vinclo vellem sociare jugali,
Postquam primus amor deceptam morte fefellit;
Si non pertæsum thalami tædæque fuisset;
Huic uni forsan potui succumbere culpæ.
Anna, fatebor enim, miseri post fata Sychæi

Rational Types   *Firmin Didot F1*

> gravi jam dudum sauci
> venis, et cæco carpitur
> virtus animo, multusqu
> os: hærent infixi pector
> nec placidam membris d

Chicago, The Newberry Library, WING ZP 739 .D563. Virgil, *Opera*. Printed in Paris, France by Pierre Didot in 1791.

The page size is 15⅛" x 10" (385 x 254 mm). The overall text measure is 7⅛" (182 mm). The book has 514 pages. The whole-page reproduction and the enlargement (two and a half times actual size) are both taken from page 215.

The achievements of the Fourniers (see *E3*) were, by the end of the 18th century, surpassed by the prodigious Didot family. More than four generations of Didots were enthusiastically involved in type making and printing. The most influential was perhaps François-Ambroise (born 1730). He was a proficient type founder and successful enough to be appointed as printer to the French royal family. It was he who ultimately refined the type measuring system, relating it to a national standard, the *pied-de-roi,* and allocating numbered sizes instead of archaic names. The Didot point system was so successful that it (eventually) received wide acceptance and is still used in Continental Europe to this day (see *Introduction*).

François-Ambroise's two sons trained in his foundry and print shop, and both of them further enhanced the reputation of the Didot family. Pierre (1761–1853) achieved international recognition for his printing; his edition of Jean Racine's *Oeuvres* was honoured in Paris (1806) and at the London Universal Exposition (1851). Firmin (1764–1836) became a punchcutter and founder whose type designs changed the course of typographic history. The brothers worked well together, and their congenial partnership is embodied in a small book published (primarily as a tribute to their father's achievements) in 1784. This *Épître sur les progrès de l'imprimerie* was written in verse by Pierre, set in new types cut by Firmin, and printed by François-Ambroise himself.

Firmin's later types are shown here in this elegant edition of Virgil's *Opera* printed by Pierre and limited to just 250 copies – another splendid example of the brothers' collaboration. This copy has the original wide margins; the pages have never been trimmed. Firmin's typeforms have very strong thick strokes and ultra-fine thin strokes; horizontal serifs which are hairline and unbracketed; and a horizontal axis on the curved letters – and these are all earmarks typical of the types once classified as 'Modern' (see also *F2* notes).

The book's extra wide margins are complemented by generous letter-, word-, and line-spacing. Firmin's **a** and **g** are a little 'squarer' than Bodoni's; and his **t** has the 'French' flat top. Note that long **s** (ſ) has now been abandoned, and short **s** is used thoughout the text.

> animo fixum immotumque

77

Quo semel est imbuta recens, servabit odorem
Testa diu. Quod si cessas, aut strenuus anteis;
Nec tardum opperior, nec praecedentibus insto.

EPISTOLA III.

AD IVLIVM FLORVM.

Iuli Flore, quibus terrarum militet oris
Claudius Augusti privignus, scire laboro.
Thracane vos, Hebrusque nivali compede vinctus;
An freta vicinas inter currentia turres,
An pingues Asiae campi, collesque morantur?
Quid studiosa cohors operum struit? hoc quoque curo.
Quis sibi res gestas Augusti scribere sumit?
Bella quis, et paces longum diffundit in aevum?
Quid Titius, Romana brevi venturus in ora,
Pindarici fontis qui non expalluit haustus,
Fastidire lacus, et rivos ausus apertos?
Vt valet? ut meminit nostri? fidibusne Latinis
Thebanos aptare modos studet, auspice Musa?
An tragica desaevit, et ampullatur in arte?

Rational Types   *Giambattista Bodoni F2*

Chicago, The Newberry Library, Wing zp 735 .b627. Horace, *Opera*. Printed in Parma, Italy by G B Bodoni, 1791.

The page size is 17½" x 11⅜" (446 x 290 mm). The overall text measure is 6⅞" (177 mm). The book has 385 pages. The whole-page reproduction is taken from page 289, the enlargement (two and a half times actual size) from page 313.

Giambattista Bodoni was born in Saluzzo in the Piedmont region of Italy in February 1740. From early childhood he was exposed to the printing trade – both his father and grandfather were active printers. When he was just 18 years old he moved to Rome to live with his uncle and to receive training at the *Tipografia della Congregazione di Propaganda Fide*. In 1766 Bodoni left Rome, planning to visit England, apparently to learn more of John Baskerville but, hindered by illness, he returned to his family in Saluzzo. In 1768, while he was there, the call came which would shape the rest of his working life. Mgr Paolo Maria Paciaudi, the head of the Duke of Parma's new library and printing press, had known Bodoni in Rome, and he arranged the appointment of Bodoni as Director of the Stamperia Ducale. No doubt the Duke's Prime Minister, Guglielmo du Tillot, was behind Parma's attempt to rival and perhaps even surpass the prestigious Imprimerie royale in Paris.

Giambattista Bodoni was a most accomplished typographer. He excelled in all aspects of the printing process. He cut punches with exacting precision and provided incredibly subtle variations of weight, width, and x-height within each size of type; he cast his types with superb accuracy, retaining the fine, hairline strokes, even at the smallest sizes; and he printed his books with meticulous care, selecting smooth *vélin* (wove) paper and rich black ink. His page designs have monumental simplicity – clearly influenced by John Baskerville (see *E5* and *E6*), whose books Bodoni greatly admired. The immense margins, huge interlinear spaces, open letter spacing, and deliberate lack of ornament all serve to enhance his sharply printed types. Opening one of Bodoni's books can be quite breathtaking, for in it we recognise the Book as Art.

The types of Bodoni quintessentially define what was once known as the 'Modern' style – letterforms with very strong thick/thin stroke contrast, horizontal axes, and hairline serifs. But their rather austere and static forms mean that 'Modern' types, when set in long text, are perhaps less comfortable to read.

Bodoni's roman type illustrated here, from the Horace of 1791, appears in the 1818 *Manuale* and named *ascendonica 3* (*c.* 22pt). His lowercase letters are very similar to those of Firmin Didot (see *F1*).

PRAEFATIO

ne quid statim occurreret, quod a mundo simplicique, quem volumus, cultu alienum videretur; statui, quantum est prolegomenon, scholiorum, et variarum lectionum ab hoc volumine prohibere: immo, si nomina demas Deorum, vel hominum, quae sibi poema quodque praescribit, ne argumenta quidem adesse passus sum; queis etsi antiquitas quaedam sit munimento, non tamen a me tanti facta sunt, ut tam venustis, tam claris poematis praeponerentur. Nostrarum vero quod erat praecipue partium egimus ita, ut haec editio primum ab orthographia, deinde a lectionum delectu, denique a stigmatum collocatione, quam maxime fieri per nos poterat, commendaretur.

Ad orthographiam quod spectat, cavimus pariter nequid nimis indiligenter, nequid curiose nimis ageremus. Quod institutum nostrum insimulabunt, opinor, nonnulli Angliae, Bataviae, Germaniae, ceterum eruditissimi viri, qui genus aliud ortho-

Rational Types   *Giambattista Bodoni*   F3

Chicago, The Newberry Library, Wing zp 735 .b627. Horace, *Opera*. Printed in Parma, Italy by G B Bodoni, 1791.

The page size is 17½" x 11⅜" (446 x 290 mm). The overall text measure is 6⅞" (177 mm). The book has 385 pages. The whole-page reproduction is taken from page ii, the enlargement (two and a half times actual size) from page vi.

In addition to the many books produced directly as a service to the Duke of Parma, Bodoni published a number of specimen books to display the new types he had created. The earliest, *Fregi e Majuscole* (1771), was heavily influenced by the designs of Fournier. A *Manuale Tipografico*, published in 1788, includes 100 different roman types, 50 italics, and 28 greeks. Bodoni made a speciality of foreign language founts, not only the usual greek and hebrew, but also many 'exotics'. The ultimate showcase for his 'exotic' faces was his *Oratio Dominica* (Lord's Prayer) printed in 1806 in 155 languages – deliberately outdoing the Imprimerie royale in Paris which had printed an *Oratio* with a mere 150 versions!

The lasting memorial to Bodoni, however, is the spectacular *Manuale Tipografico* published five years after his death in 1818. His widow, Margherita, helped by Luigi Orsi (his long-serving foreman), painstakingly completed Giambattista's magnificent specimen of types. This beautifully printed *Manuale* is astonishing not only for its immensity of range, but also for its incredible detail. Two huge volumes carry 538 pages of type specimens – the first one alone has 142 different roman types. There are 22 different sizes of type shown, ranging from *parmigianina* (*c.* 5pt) to *papale* (*c.* 72pt). Within each size there are numerous subtle variations of weight, letter width, and x-height – the *testo* size (*c.* 18pt), for example, has 14 separate versions. Bodoni himself calculated that a single roman fount needed 196 separate punches. Today, the Museo Bodoniano in Parma has in safe keeping more than 22,500 of his letter punches!

The design of Bodoni's italic typefaces varies considerably. Quite apart from the cursive founts designed to stand alone, the 142 italic faces he cut to accompany his roman types have many distinctly different features. The italic shown here, with its 'swash' capitals, strong forward slant, and open letter spacing could perhaps be described as a 'semi-cursive' style. It appears (without the 'swash' caps) in the *Manuale* of 1818 and named *palestina 6* (*c.* 24pt). The ascenders and descenders are seriffed, but the entrance strokes on **i**, **m**, **n**, and **u** are 'hooked'. The **a** is rather wide, but the **m** is narrow.

81

GREAT PRIMER, No. 3.

Breathes there the man, with soul so dead,
Who never to himself hath said,
   This is my own, my native land!
Whose heart hath ne'er within him burned,
As home his footsteps he hath turned,
   From wandering on a foreign strand!
If such there breathe, go, mark him well;
For him no Minstrel raptures swell;
High though his titles, proud his name,
Boundless his wealth as wish can claim;
Despite those titles, power, and pelf,
The wretch, concentered all in self,
Living, shall forfeit fair renown,
And, doubly dying, shall go down
To the vile dust, from whence he sprung,
Unwept, unhonoured, and unsung.

   O Caledonia! stern and wild,
Meet nurse for a poetic child!
Land of brown heath and shaggy wood,
Land of the mountain and the flood,
Land of my sires! what mortal hand
Can e'er untie the filial band,
That knits me to thy rugged strand!
Still as I view each well known scene,
Think what is now, and what hath been,

ALEX. WILSON & SONS.

Nineteenth-century Types *Richard Austin G1*

> y own, my native lan
> t hath ne'er within hi
> s footsteps he hath tur
> ndering on a foreign s
> e breathe, go, mark hi

Chicago, The Newberry Library, CASE WING z 40543 .9722. Alexander Wilson & Sons, *Specimen of Modern Printing Types*. Printed in Glasgow, Scotland in 1833.

The page size is 11½" x 9" (292 x 228 mm). The overall text measure is 4⅝" (109 mm). The book has 167 unnumbered folios. The whole-page reproduction and the enlargement (three and a half times actual size) are both taken from the '*Great Primer, No 3*' page.

Richard Austin was born in London in August 1756, and he apprenticed to John Phillips, a seal engraver and punchcutter, when he was just 14 years old. Austin is perhaps best-known for the fine types he cut for John Bell from 1788 onwards, but he also cut greek types for Cambridge University Press during the years 1808–1810. These were based on the designs of the classical scholar Richard Porson, and the greek typeface *Porson* became *the* standard for all classical and New Testament texts published in England for well over 100 years. Until the recent extensive researches of Alastair Johnston, however, very little else was known about Austin or the hugely influential rôle he played in the development of later type design (see Johnston, *Transitional Faces*).

In the wake of the radical type designs of Didot and Bodoni (see *F1–F3*), their 'Modern' style became the norm for 19th-century printing. But Austin's new types, cut for two Scottish foundries, were deliberately less austere and more practical. These types appeared in the Wilson & Sons specimen of 1812 and that of William Miller of 1813. T C Hansard's statement (in *Typographia*, 1825) that Austin cut types for both companies at the same time, could be thought odd, but Johnston points out that, in addition to other evidence, the *Pica Roman No 1* which Austin shows in the 1819 specimen of his own Imperial Letter Foundry is virtually indistinguishable from the *New Pica Roman No 2* in Miller's specimen of 1822.

These types of Austin were later imported into the United States by the Samuel Dickinson Foundry of Boston from the Edinburgh firm of Wilsons and Sinclair. Dickinson showed them in his 1847 specimen and praised these 'Scotch Faces' for their quality, durability, and *cheapness*. So it was that the types derived from those of Richard Austin became known as *Scotch Roman*.

This *great primer* typeface (*c.* 18pt) is the same as that shown in the earlier Wilson & Sons specimen of 1812. Austin's letters are sharply cut, with rounded forms and carefully balanced thick and thin strokes. His capitals are the same height as the ascenders. Note the sensitively bracketed serifs, replacing the fragile hairlines of Didot and Bodoni.

> dless his wealth as wish can claim

83

ENGLISH CLARENDON ON GREAT PRIMER BODY.
Cast to range with ordinary Great Primer, the Figures to En Quadrats.

PIRACY is the great sin of all **manufacturing communities**:—there is scarcely any Trade in which it prevails so generally as among **TYPE FOUNDERS. Messrs. BESLEY & Co.** originally introduced the **Clarendon Character,** which they registered under the **Copyright of Designs' Act,** but no sooner was the time of Copyright allowed by that Act **expired,** than the **Trade was inundated** with all sorts of **Piracies and Imitations,** some of them **mere effigies of letters.** Notwithstanding this, nearly all the **respectable Printers in Town and Country** who claim to have either **taste** or **judgment,** have adopted the **original Founts,** and treated the Imitations with the contempt they deserve.

SMALL PICA CLARENDON ON PICA BODY.
Cast to range with ordinary Pica, the Figures to En Quadrats.

PIRACY is the great sin of all **manufacturing communities:**—there is scarcely any Trade in which it prevails so generally as among **Type Founders. Messrs. BESLEY & COMPANY** originally introduced the **Clarendon Character,** which they registered under the **Copyright of Designs' Act,** but no sooner was the time of Copyright allowed by that Act **expired,** than the **Trade was inundated** with all sorts of **Piracies** and **Imitations,** some of them **mere effigies of letters.** Notwithstanding this, nearly all the **respectable Printers in Town and Country** who claim to have either **taste** or **judgment,** have adopted the original Founts, and treated the **Imitations** with the contempt they deserve.

LONG PRIMER CLARENDON ON SMALL PICA BODY.
Cast to range with ordinary Small Pica, the Figures to En Quadrats.

PIRACY is the great sin of all **manufacturing communities :**—there is scarcely any Trade in which it prevails so generally as among **TYPE FOUNDERS. Messrs. R. BESLEY & Co.** originally introduced the **Clarendon Character,** which they registered under the **Copyright of Designs' Act,** but no sooner was the time of Copyright allowed by that Act **expired,** than the **Trade was inundated** with all sorts of **Piracies** and **Imitations,** some of them **mere effigies of letters.** Notwithstanding this, nearly all the **respectable Printers in Town and Country** who claim to have either **taste** or **judgment,** have adopted the original Founts, and treated the **Imitations** with the contempt they deserve.

R. BESLEY AND CO., LONDON.

Nineteenth-century Types   *Robert Besley* G2

> atilina, patientia no
> e tuus eludet? que
> ; audacia? nihilne t
> nihilne urbis vigiliæ
> s bonorum omnium

Chicago, The Newberry Library, Wing z 40545 .093. Fann Street Letter Foundry, *A General Specimen of Printing Types*. Printed in London, England most likely in 1857.

The page size is 11¼" x 8½" (287 x 216 mm). The text measure is 4⅝" (148 mm). The book has 214 unnumbered folios. The enlargement (three times actual size) is taken from the '*Double Pica Clarendon*' sample.

Bold-face types were first seen in large sizes, appropriate for advertising. Such display founts as 'fat-faces' (exaggerated, obese 'Bodoni-like' styles) appeared as early as 1810, and heavy slab-serif types (confusingly called 'Antique' by Figgins and 'Egyptian' by Thorowgood), were common by 1820. However, Michael Twyman points out that it was not until around 1838 that smaller sizes of these bold types were used in books, usually for chronological charts or tables.

In 1845 Robert Besley introduced his innovative series of *Clarendon* types in his Fann Street specimen. These were the very first bold-faces specifically designed to be set within normal roman text type. These types, said Besley, were made with great care, avoiding 'the clumsy inelegance' of earlier attempts to combine slab-serif 'Antiques' with roman text.

Robert Besley, born in Exeter in 1794, joined the foundry of Thorowgood & Co when he was just 32 years old. By 1838 he had been appointed a partner in the firm, and when William Thorowgood retired in 1849, the company became 'Besley & Co'. The punchcutter at the foundry was Benjamin Fox. Talbot Baines Reed, a later director of the continuing firm, considered him to be 'a practical and skilled punchcutter'. Fox was responsible for cutting the *Clarendon* series, perhaps working to Besley's designs.

The Designs Copyright Act was extended in 1839. Besley was perhaps the first to obtain copyright protection for a typeface. But his 1845 *Clarendon* designs proved so popular that as soon as the three years of copyright had expired, every English typefounder raced to produce his own version.

Robert Besley's righteous indignation at this 'piracy' can be felt in the paragraphs he printed in the 1857 Specimen (see opposite). He not only denounces their plagiarism, but also berates the miserable results of the imitators. Incidentally, these paragraphs demonstrate how well *Clarendon* could be used within roman text, to achieve a nicely judged emphasis.

The fine quality of Benjamin Fox's cutting is apparent in the enlarged detail of his *double pica* (c. 20pt) *Clarendon* type (above). This bold face, although slightly condensed, is not too heavy. His letters retain a lot of individual character and even a certain liveliness – note the lowercase **b** and **g**, and the 'cupping' of the upper slab-bracketed serifs. The x-height is large, and the counter shapes are open.

> furor iste tuus eludet? qu

85

Great Primer Old Style.

TYPE of the old style of face is now frequently uſed—more eſpecially for the finer claſs of book work; as however the faces which were cut in the early part of the laſt century are now unpleaſing both to the eye of the critic and to the general reader, on account of their inequality of *ſize* and conſequent irregularity of *ranging*, the Subſcribers have been induced to produce this ſeries, in which they have endeavoured to avoid the objectionable peculiarities, whilſt retaining the diſtinctive characteriſtics of the mediæval letters. The ſeries is complete from Double Pica to Pearl, with all the intermediate bodies, and has Roman and Italic Accents to each fount.

Miller & Richard.

Nineteenth-century Types   *Alexander Phemister* G3

> their inequality of
> irregularity of *rangi*
> have been induced to
> in which they have e
> the objectionable pe

Chicago, The Newberry Library, WING Z 40543 .5733. Miller & Richard, *Specimen of Old Style Types*. Printed in Edinburgh, Scotland in 1868.

The page size is 10⅞" x 7¾" (275 x 197 mm). The text measure is 4⅛" (105 mm). The book has 22 unnumbered folios. The whole-page reproduction and the enlargement (three and a half times actual size) are both taken from the 'Great Primer Old Style' page.

Born in Edinburgh in 1829, Alexander Phemister served an apprenticeship with a noted punchcutter of the time, William Grandison, graduating at the age of 23. His first employment was with the Edinburgh type foundry of Miller & Richard. In their specimen of 1860, they published a series of *Old Style* faces cut for them by Phemister. These new types were much admired (and soon copied!) by most other British foundries. Phemister's designs had a significant influence on subsequent type design and, as a result of his work, Miller & Richard gained international recognition. William E Loy points out that Alexander Phemister was one of the few punchcutters in those days who designed as well as cut his own alphabets.

In 1861 Phemister emigrated to the United States, and after working for two years with the New York firm of George Bruce & Son, he moved to the Dickinson Type Foundry in Boston. For them he cut a modified version of his Miller & Richard face, naming it *Franklin Old Style*.

Following the Chiswick Press revival of the old face types of Caslon in the mid 1840s (see *D7* notes), there was a growing dissatisfaction with the austere 'Bodoni-like' types and an inclination to return to the more congenial styles of Aldus, Garamont, and Caslon. In their 1868 Type Specimen (see opposite), Miller & Richard boasted that their *Old Style* faces met this need and, in fact, were better than the older types because they avoided the 'objectional peculiarities… of the mediaeval letters'! Miller & Richard imported the David Bruce casting machine from America in 1849, so it is likely that these types were mechanically cast.

The *great primer* (*c.* 16pt) *Old Style* letters shown here retain the bracketed, angled serifs of the old faces, but the letter strokes are much lighter and, unlike old faces, the axis is clearly horizontal. Compared to Caslon, some capitals are narrower, **P** and **R** are a little wider, and lowercase **a** and **e** are more open. Note Phemister's distinctive **g**, and the very low branching on his italic **h**, **n**, and **r**. The long s (ſ) and ct and ſt ligatures are no doubt included in order to promote the supposed antique character of the type.

> intermediate bodies, and has Ron

87

And on her hot hands, and her tear-stained face,
Half-fainting, the pine-scented air she felt,
And all about the salt sea savour smelt,
And in her ears the dashing of the sea
Rang ever; thus the God had set her free.

BUT by the shore further they led her still
To where the sea beat on a barren hill,
And a long stage of timber met the sea,
At end whereof was tossing fearfully
A little boat that had no oars or sail,
Or aught that could the mariner avail.
Thither with her their steps the soldiers bent,
And as along the narrow way they went
The salt waves leapt aloft to kiss her feet
And in the wind streamed out her tresses sweet;
But little heed she took of feet or head,
For nought she doubted she to death was led,
But ever did she hold against her breast
The little babe, and spoke not for the rest;
No, not when in the boat they bade her go,
And 'twixt its bulwarks thin she lay alow,
Nor when adrift they set her presently
And all about was but the angry sea.

NO word she said until the sun was down,
And she beheld the moon that on no town,
On no fair homestead, no green pasture shone,
But lit up the unwearied sea alone;
No word she said till she was far from shore
And on her breast the babe was wailing sore;
And then she lifted up her face to Jove,
And said: O thou who once didst call me love,
Hast thou forgotten those fair words of thine,

The Doom of King Acrisius

Private Press Types   *William Morris   H1*

Chicago, The Newberry Library, WING ZP 845 .K336. William Morris, *The Earthly Paradise*. Printed at the Kelmscott Press in Hammersmith, England in 1896.

The page size is 9¼" x 6½" (235 x 168 mm). The overall text measure is 4" (101 mm). The book is in eight volumes with a total of 1560 pages. The whole page reproduction is taken from volume 2, page 21, and the enlargement (four and a half times actual size) is from volume 2, page 25.

William Morris' early interest in letterforms and book design was suddenly brought into sharp focus at a slide lecture given by Emery Walker on 15 November 1888. The greatly enlarged screen images of 15th-century typefaces so captured Morris' imagination that on the way home with Walker he exclaimed, 'Let's make a fount of type'. This interaction between two friends eventually led to the establishing of the Kelmscott Press in 1890 and the making of its *Golden* type. Morris moved the Press to Upper Mall in Hammersmith in 1891, next door to Emery Walker's Process Engaving firm.

They both much admired the types of Nicolas Jenson (see *B2*), so for the new design Emery Walker provided photo enlargements of his 1470s types and also some of Aretino's *Historiae Florentini populi* printed by Jacobus Rubeus in 1476, whose type closely resembles Jenson's. Morris studied these enlargements with great care, tracing over them many times. But then he drew his own letters, capturing 'the essence' rather than copying the originals. He himself admitted that his *Golden* type, 'especially in the lowercase, tends rather more to the gothic than does Jenson's'. The type got its name is from *The Golden Legend*, which was intended to be the first book from the Kelmscott Press.

William Morris designed a second fount, *Troy* (an 18pt gothic rotunda) and a 12pt version of that called *Chaucer*. The punches for all three Kelmscott types were expertly cut by Edward Prince, who cut the punches for the Doves Press and also for the Ashendene (see *H2* and *H3*).

The quality and style of the Kelmscott Press books caused a sensation in the printing world at the time. Numerous private presses emerged in its wake, and the Kelmscott types were much imitated. But the rather 'medieval' look of their books was not universally admired. Cobden-Sanderson, of the Doves Press, was one of the few people at the time to openly criticise the heaviness of the *Golden* type. Stanley Morison, in private correspondence, considered it to be 'positively foul'(!), but publically he acknowledged Morris' superb craftsmanship and his remarkable attention to detail.

William Morris died in October 1896, and within two years the Kelmscott Press closed. Perhaps Morris' legacy lies not so much in the design of his type, nor in the look of his pages, but in the absolute integrity of his work. Ultimately it was this which inspired improvements in printing, even in the commercial trade.

In *The Earthly Paradise* shown here, the boldness of the 14pt *Golden* type is actually well-matched with Morris' characteristically gothic initials. The thin strokes of the type are very heavy (lowercase **o** is almost monoline). Compare *Golden* with the earlier *Clarendon* of Robert Besley *(G2)*.

THE ANGEL ENDED, AND IN
    ADAMS EARE
  SO CHARMING LEFT HIS VOICE,
    THAT HE A WHILE
Thought him still speaking, still stood fixt to hear;
Then as new wak't thus gratefully repli'd.
What thanks sufficient, or what recompence
Equal have I to render thee, Divine
Hystorian, who thus largely hast allayd
The thirst I had of knowledge, and voutsaf't
This friendly condescention to relate
Things else by me unsearchable, now heard
With wonder, but delight, and, as is due,
With glorie attributed to the high
Creator; some thing yet of doubt remaines,
Which onely thy solution can resolve.
When I behold this goodly Frame, this World
Of Heav'n and Earth consisting, and compute,
Thir magnitudes, this Earth a spot, a graine,
An Atom, with the Firmament compar'd
And all her numberd Starrs, that seem to rowle
Spaces incomprehensible (for such
Thir distance argues and thir swift return
Diurnal) meerly to officiate light
Round this opacous Earth, this punctual spot,
One day and night; in all thir vast survey
Useless besides, reasoning I oft admire,
How Nature wise and frugal could commit
Such disproportions, with superfluous hand

Private Press Types   *T J Cobden-Sanderson*   H2

e Oracle of God; I then
y aid to my adventrous
no middle flight intend
Aonian Mount, while
attempted yet in Prose

Chicago, The Newberry Library, WING ZP 945 .D7408. John Milton, *Paradise Lost.* Printed at the Doves Press in Hammersmith, England in 1902.

The page size is 9¼" x 6½" (235 x 165 mm). The overall text measure is 4" (102 mm). The book has 388 pages. The whole page reproduction is taken from page 230, and the enlargement (four times actual size) is from page 16.

Thomas James Sanderson, born in December 1840, was for a while a lawyer at Lincoln's Inn. After his marriage to Annie Cobden (he added her surname to his), he trained as a fine bookbinder. In 1893 he set up the Doves Bindery (named after the local pub!) in Hammersmith, across the street from Kelmscott House where William Morris lived.

From the outset, he was interested in the printing as well as the binding of books, and by 1900 he had established the Doves Press. Cobden-Sanderson had very specific aims for the books produced by his Press. In *The Book Beautiful*, published in 1901, he outlined his ideals of clarity of type, unobtrusiveness of decoration, and appropriateness of binding, all in harmony with each other – and the whole reflecting the order and beauty of the universe!

• The Doves Press began as a partnership. Emery Walker, previously an advisor to William Morris, provided Cobden-Sanderson with a great deal of expertise in technical aspects of typography and printing. For the design of the new *Doves* type, Walker wanted it to be 'the closest copy I could make or get made of Nicolas Jenson's type' (compare B2). But neither of the partners were capable of making the drawings,

so Emery Walker recruited Percy Tiffin from his own Photo Engraving company to trace over the photo enlargements of Aretino's *Historiae Florentini populi* that he had already made for Morris. These he supplemented with capitals taken from a Jenson imprint, the Pliny of 1476. Edward Prince was then commissioned to cut the punches for the *Doves* type.

The partnership between Cobden-Sanderson and Emery Walker was not an easy one – they had radically different aspirations for the Doves Press. Things became so strained that the partnership was dissolved in 1909, and thereafter Emery Walker's name was removed from the colophons of the books. A legal wrangle ensued. Walker was given the right to some of the *Doves* type once the Press closed, but in 1917, after printing his last book, Cobden-Sanderson threw all the punches, matrices, and remaining type into the River Thames, spitefully denying Walker's claim on them.

From 1900 until 1917 the Doves Press published 40 books, most of them bound in limp vellum at the Doves Bindery. The book illustrated here was the first major work of the Press. A W Pollard concluded that there was 'no more perfect book in roman type'. Note the huge margins, the precisely printed text in the striking *c.*16pt *Doves* roman, and the careful use of calligraphic initials. Edward Johnston wrote an imposing heading for the opening page, which was engraved by C E Keates, and printed in vermilion. The large blue T on page 230 was handwritten by Graily Hewitt.

Creator; some thing yet of doubt rema

91

Canto Decimosecondo.

SI TOSTO come l'ultima parola
    La benedetta fiamma per dir tolse,
    A rotar cominciò la santa mola;
E nel suo giro tutta non si volse
    Prima ch'un'altra di cerchio la chiuse,
    E moto a moto, e canto a canto colse;
Canto, che tanto vince nostre Muse,
    Nostre Sirene, in quelle dolci tube,
    Quanto primo splendor quel ch'ei refuse.
Come si volgon per tenera nube
    Due archi paralleli e concolori,
    Quando Junone a sua ancella iube,
Nascendo di quel d'entro quel di fuori,
    A guisa del parlar di quella vaga,
    Ch'amor consunse come sol vapori;
E fanno qui la gente esser presaga,
    Per lo patto che Dio con Noè pose,
    Del mondo che giammai più non si allaga:
Così di quelle sempiterne rose
    Volgeansi circa noi le due ghirlande,
    E sì l'estrema all'ultima rispose.

> chi regnar per forza o per s
> rubare, e chi civil negozio,
> i nel diletto della carne in
> affaticava, e chi si dava all
> do da tutte queste cose sc

Chicago, The Newberry Library, WING ZP 945 .A822. Alighieri Dante, *Lo Paradiso*. Printed at the Ashendene Press in Chelsea, England in 1905.

The page size is 8" x 5½" (201 x 140 mm). The overall text measure is 3¼" (82 mm). The book has 244 pages. The whole-page reproduction is taken from page 82, the enlargement (three and a half times actual size) from page 75.

The setting up of the Kelmscott Press in 1891 stimulated wide interest in fine printing. A number of other private presses followed, the most distinguished being the Doves Press and the Ashendene. Both of these benefitted a great deal from the earlier experiments of William Morris, in his relentless pursuit of excellence in printing. They obtained paper and ink from the same manufacturers discovered by Walker and Morris, and their books were printed on the same type of handpress that they used, the Albion. Even more significant, two craftsmen were closely involved in the work of all three presses. Emery Walker not only provided expert technical advice to them all, but also large-scale photographs of 15th-century typefaces to aid in the design of their new types. The very skilful punchcutter Edward Prince cut the types for Ashendene as well as for Kelmscott and Doves.

In 1894 Charles Henry St John (pronounced 'Sin-jun') Hornby established a private press at his father's home at Ashendene in Hertfordshire. At first he used commercially available founts but, six years later, having moved the press to Chelsea, he resolved to create his own typeface. Advised by Emery Walker and Sydney Cockerell (William Morris'

secretary), Hornby decided to base it on the 'fere-humanistica' type used by Sweynheym and Pannartz, in the monastery at Subiaco, for their 1465 Lactantius (see *B1*). Undoubtedly, Emery Walker provided large-scale photographs, traced as a guide for the new typeface, which Hornby named *Subiaco*. It was only cut in *great primer* size (c. 18pt) but was the main type used for Ashendene Press publications from 1902 until it finally closed in 1935.

The design of the books from Ashendene are elegantly austere, with little or no extraneous decoration. They have large margins, carefully set type, and are beautifully printed. Stanley Morison considered them to be 'a spectacular achievement'. In the early editions, Graily Hewitt added coloured initials by hand; in later ones these were printed from engravings of Hewitt's handwritten letters.

The book illustrated here, the Dante of 1905, uses the *Subiaco* type with great style. Graily Hewitt's vigorous, handwritten initial **S** in green contrasts perfectly with the strong black text. Many of the idiosyncratic features of the original Sweynheym and Pannartz type have been retained in the Ashendene version, except for the long **s** (ſ), the flourished **ct**, and the Latin abbreviations. Compare the original type (see *B1*) with this one. They are practically indistinguishable. Note the ligatures for **fi**, **fu**, **ti**, and **tu** in the Ashendene type.

> Quando Junone a sua ancella iube,

Glossary

Ampersand Symbol for the Latin word *et*, meaning 'and'.

Ascenders The strokes of certain lowercase letters, like b, f, and h, which project above the midline.

Axis The angle at which the thickest part of a shaded curved stroke is drawn in relationship to the horizontal.

Baseline The perceived line on which most capital and lowercase letters appear to rest. Descending strokes of letters like J, Q, g, p, and y break through the baseline.

Bâtarde A letterform deriving from a cursive gothic hand which first appeared in late 15th century manuscripts of northern France. (See *Historical Scripts, D6*.)

Bifolium (*pl.* bifolia) Two folios, joined, making four pages.

Blackletter General term used to describe scripts and types of the gothic period. Heavy weight, often angular in form, and compressed. Typical examples are textura and bâtarde.

Body size In metal type, the depth of the shank of metal on which the face of the type sits. It measures, at a minimum, from the top of the lowercase ascenders to the bottom of the descenders. Body size is usually expressed in points.

Bracketed A serif form which incorporates a curve between the upright stroke and its horizontal ending.

c. An abbreviation for *circa*, meaning 'approximately'. Most commonly used for dates.

Cap An abbreviation for 'capital' (see Uppercase).

Chase A metal frame in which type matter and illustration blocks (if needed), are locked up for printing (see Forme).

Codex Book form made up of several quires, sewn together.

Colophon Tailpiece, summary, or printer's device at the end of a printed book, often giving details of date, place, and manner of production.

Composition sizes Type sizes used for text setting (or 'body matter'), commonly ranging from 6pt to 14pt body size.

Contraction An abbreviation for an omitted syllable at the beginning or in the middle of a word (see *A1* notes).

Counters The internal white spaces within a letterform.

Counterpunch A special stamp, used in the early stages of punchcutting, to impress the counter shape of a letter into the face of the punch.

Cursive In typography, a script-style of type, often sloped, and in imitation of similar calligraphic hands.

Descenders The strokes of certain lowercase letters, like g, p, and q which fall below the baseline.

Display sizes Type sizes used for display setting (for title pages, chapter headings, or advertising material), commonly ranging from 14pt to 72pt body size.

Drop cap Large initial capital letter, inserted into a deliberately indented space at the beginning of a book or chapter.

Earmarks Particular features or unique characteristics of a typeface which help distinguish it from other, similar faces.

Epigraphic Pertaining to inscriptional letters carved in stone or engraved in metal.

Extenders Overall term for both ascenders and descenders.

Face The typeface. The inked surface of metal type which comes in contact with the paper. Thus, the printed form of the letter; also used to denote the design of a particular type.

Folio One leaf of a book. Two pages, one recto (right hand) and one verso (left hand).

Foredge margin The outside margin of a page.

Forme The complete type matter, illustration blocks (if needed), and spacing material, locked up with quoins in a chase, ready for printing.

Foundry In typographic terms, the workshop or factory where letterpress type is cast.

Fount (or 'font') A complete set of type characters of one particular size and style, comprising letters, figures, and punctuation marks. In modern use, it also means 'typeface'.

Full point The punctuation mark for 'full stop', or 'period'.

Gathering See Quire.

Gloss A translation or commentary, often printed in the margin, or between the lines of the main text.

Glyph An individual character from a typeface, see Sort.

Gothic Of the Goths. Originally coined as a term of derision for what was perceived as the 'barbaric' art of northern and western Europe. In lettering it refers to heavy, often angular, scripts commonly used during the late 12th to late 15th centuries, like textura or rotunda. In the 19th century it was, confusingly, also used to denote sans-serifs.

Grotesque A British term sometimes used as an alternative to the American use of 'gothic' to denote sans-serif types.

Hairline Part of a letter which is an extremely thin stroke. Eg, a hairline serif; commonly horizontal and unbracketed.

Head margin The upper margin of a page.

Height-to-paper The height of a piece of cast metal type from its base to its printing face. Each sort, or illustration block, must have precisely the same height-to-paper to ensure evenness of inking and printing.

Humanist Pertaining to the Renaissance period. Term used especially of Italian scholars, scribes, and printers.

Illuminator A professional decorator of manuscripts and printed books. 'Illumination' originally signified the use of gold or silver to 'light up' the page. Now used to refer to all kinds of book decoration.

Indulgence A Letter or Certificate, issued by the Catholic Church, acknowledging a donation or financial gift which, if given with 'due piety', promised forgiveness of sins.

Initial In typography and calligraphy, the first letter of a word, sentence, or paragraph often distinguished by size, colour, or decoration.

Interlinear space Denotes the amount of vertical space separating the lines of text.

Italic In typography and calligraphy, letters which are cursive in character, often forward-sloping and condensed. Originally they were stand-alone typefaces, used for 'pocket' books (see *B5* notes). Now they are mainly auxiliary types, providing emphasis or contrast within roman text setting.

Justification, justifying In typography, the spacing of words and letters to achieve text lines of equal length. Also, the process of refining a strike to form a matrix for casting type.

Kern, kerning Originally, that part of a metal sort which overhangs its shank to allow it to be set closer to adjacent letters. Especially needed in italic letters like *f* and long s (*ſ*). In modern use, 'kerning' simply refers to the fine spacing of adjoining pairs of letters.

Leading Originally, extra strips of metal (lead alloy) inserted between the lines of type to increase the interlinear space. In modern use often used, confusingly, to denote the measurement from the baseline of one line of text to the baseline of the next line.

Letterspacing Extra spacing between individual capital letters for decorative, aesthetic purposes, or in order to justify them. Lowercase letters should rarely be letterspaced.

Ligature In typography, physically linked letterforms, like fi and ffi. In metal type they would be formed as a single sort. Latin, *ligo*, 'to tie', 'to bind'.

Lowercase Small letters, as distinct from capital forms. For example, a, d, m, p, and x. These sorts were originally held in the type case located below another, hence: 'lower case'. In calligraphy, they are often called minuscule letters.

Majuscules In calligraphy, capital forms as distinct from minuscules (see Uppercase).

Matrix (*pl*, matrices) A mould, usually made of copper, created from the strike of a punch. The matrix, inserted into the adjustable mould, enables the casting of the sorts of type. (See *Introduction, Fig. 1*.)

Measure The consistent width of the lines of typesetting, usually expressed in picas. The composing stick for setting lines of metal type is fixed at the measure required. In setting uneven lines of poetry, a maximum measure is determined, and the ends of short text lines filled with quads.

Midline The perceived line which establishes the height of most lowercase letters. All capitals, and ascending strokes of letters like b, d, h, and k, break through the midline.

Minuscules In calligraphy, small letters, as distinct from majuscules (see Lowercase).

Mise-en-page The design and layout of the page. The aesthetic arrangement of the various elements on the page.

Mould The adjustable mould is a vital piece of equipment used to cast the sorts of metal type, maintaining consistent body size and height-to-paper of the type, while allowing for different widths for individual letters, like i and w.

Palaeotypography The study of the history and development of printed books and typefaces.

Pica A standard unit of measurement in typography, equalling 12 points. In the Anglo-American system it measured 0.166044 of an inch. In digital typesetting, 6 picas are rounded up to exactly one inch.

Point The smallest unit of measurement in typography, one-twelfth of a pica. In the Anglo-American system 72 points, or 6 picas, measured 0.996264 of an inch. In digital typesetting 72 points are rounded up to exactly one inch.

pt Abbreviation for 'point'.

Punch (archaic, 'puncheon') A steel tool with a letterform engraved at the end in relief, used to create a strike in copper, which is then justified to form the matrix from which metal sorts can be cast. (See *Introduction, Fig. 1*.)

Quad (archaic, 'quadrat') Metal spacing material, the exact square of the body size being set. It is shorter than the height-to-paper of the typeface so that it does not print.

Quire A set of bifolia making up one 'section' (or 'signature') sewn into a codex book. Also called a 'gathering'. For example, 4 bifolia (16 pages) might make one quire.

Quoin An adjustable wedge which is used to securely lock the type matter into a chase, so that it can be moved and positioned onto the press.

Recto (abbreviation, 'R') The top side of a folio or leaf of a document. Any right hand page.

Renaissance The period of intellectual and artistic revival, spanning the late 14th to late 16th centuries, marked by a renewal of interest in ancient, classical culture. French, *renâitre*, 'to be born anew'.

Rotunda In typography and calligraphy, gothic letterforms with a rounded aspect. Derived from manuscript hands of the late 15th and early 16th centuries, mainly from Italy and Spain. (See *Historical Scripts, F1*.)

Roman In typography, the name given to typefaces which were derived from Humanist minuscule scripts of the 15th century. Now simply used to denote upright, seriffed types.

Rubricator A scribe who completed printed books and manuscripts by adding initials, chapter headings, and other texts in colour, especially red. Latin, *rubrica*, 'red'.

Sans-serif Literally, 'without serifs'. Letterforms which have no serifs, and which often appear to be monoline (having little or no distinction between their thick and thin strokes).

Serif (archaic, 'ceriph' or 'surryph') A finishing cross-stroke added to the ends of main strokes of letters. Often considered to be an aid in reading. Serifs are generally bracketed, hairline, or slab. The origin of the word is obscure. Harry Carter (1968) suggested that it may derive from the Dutch, *schreef*, meaning a 'scratch' or 'flick of the pen'.

Shading The modulation from thin to thick, especially in curved letter strokes.

Slab A form of serif which is rectangular and rather heavy. These may also be bracketed (see *G2*).

Sort An individual piece of cast metal type, carrying a single character – a letter, figure, punctuation, symbol, or ligature in one style and size. (See *Introduction, Fig. 1*.)

Strike The initial impression made by a punch in a piece of copper. When justified, the strike forms the matrix from which the individual sorts of type are cast in the mould. (See *Introduction, Fig. 1*.)

Suspension An abbreviation for an omitted syllable at the end of a word (see *A1* notes).

Tail margin The lower margin of a page.

Text sizes Type sizes used for text setting (or 'body matter'), commonly ranging from 6pt to 14pt body size.

Textura A gothic letterform with strong angular aspect and tight lateral compression. Derived from northern European manuscript hands of the late 13th to 15th centuries. (See *Historical Scripts, D5*.)

Typeface See Face.

Uppercase Capital letters, as distinct from lowercase forms. For example, A, D, M, P, and X. These sorts were originally held in the type case located above another, hence: 'upper case'. In calligraphy, they are often called majuscule letters.

Vellum Animal skin prepared for writing or printing. Sometimes called parchment.

Verso (abbreviation 'v') The underside of a folio or leaf of a document. Any left hand page.

Weight In typography and calligraphy, the relationship between the width of the main strokes and the overall height of the letterform.

x-height The height of lowercase letters, like a, m, o, and x, which do not have ascenders or descenders. The x-height is the distance from the midline to the baseline.

Select Bibliography

General

Bartram, Alan: *Typeforms, a history*, Oak Knoll Press/The British Library, New Castle/London, 2007

Bringhurst, Robert: *The Elements of Typographic Style*, Hartley & Marks, Vancouver, 1997

Blumenthal, Joseph: *Art of the Printed Book, 1455–1955*, The Pierpont Morgan Library/David R Godine, Boston, 1984

Carter, Harry: *A View of Early Typography, up to about 1600*, intro by James Mosley, Hyphen Press, London, 2002

Chappel, Warren and Robert Bringhurst: *A Short History of the Printed Word*, Hartley & Marks, Vancouver, 1999

De Vinne, Theodore L, *Plain Printing Types, a treatise on the processes of type-making, the point system, the names, sizes, and styles of types*, Oswald Publishing, New York, 1914

Dowding, Geoffrey: *An Introduction to the History of Printing Types*, Oak Knoll Press/The British Library, New Castle/London, 1998

Knight, Stan: 'The Roman Alphabet', article in *The World's Writing Systems*, ed. Peter T Daniels and William Bright, Oxford University Press, New York, 1996

Knight, Stan: *Historical Scripts*, Oak Knoll Press, New Castle, 2003

Lawson, Alexander with Dwight Agner: *Printing Types*, Beacon Press, Boston, 1990

Lawson, Alexander: *Anatomy of a Typeface*, David R Godine, Boston, 2002

McLean, Ruari: *Manual of Typography*, Thames and Hudson, London, 1992

McLean, Ruari: *How Typography Happens*, Oak Knoll Press/The British Library, New Castle/London, 2000

Morison, Stanley: *Four Centuries of Fine Printing*, Ernest Benn, London, 1949

Morison, Stanley: *A Tally of Types*, ed. Brooke Crutchley, Cambridge University Press, Cambridge, 1973

Mosley, James: *Le 'Point IN'*, unpublished paper, London, 1997

Mosley, James: *Notes on the Origin of the Point System*, unpublished paper, London, 2007

Moxon, Joseph: *Mechanick Exercises on the Whole Art of Printing*, ed. Herbert Davis and Harry Carter, Dover, New York, 1978

Smeijers, Fred: *Counterpunch*, ed. Robin Kinross, Hyphen Press, London, 1996

Steinberg, S H: *Five Hundred Years of Printing*, rev. by John Trevitt, Oak Knoll Press/The British Library, New Castle/London, 1996

Sutton, James and Alan Bartram: *An Atlas of Typeforms*, Chartwell Books, New Jersey, 1988

Tracy, Walter: *Letters of Credit, a view of type design*, David R Godine, Boston, 1986

Twyman, Michael: *The British Library Guide to Printing, history and techniques*, The British Library, London, 1998

Updike, Daniel Berkeley: *Printing Types, their history, forms, and use*, Harvard University Press, Cambridge MA, 1951

Printing and the Mind of Man, Catalogue of Exhibitions at the British Museum and Earls Court, London, July 1963

The Times Newspaper: *Printing Number*, London, 10 September 1912

The Times Newspaper: *Printing Number*, London, 29 October 1929

Medieval Types

Baldasso, Renzo: 'La Stampa del'editio princeps degli Elementi di Euclide', article in *The Books of Venice (Il libro veneziano)*, Oak Knoll, Delaware, 2009

Boardley, John: 'Erhard Ratdolt', article in *Codex, the journal of typography*, Yokohama, Issue 01, Spring 2011

Conway, Melissa: *The diaro of the printing press of San Jacopo di Ripoli 1476–1484*, Olschki, Florence, 1999

Davies, Martin: *The Gutenberg Bible*, Pomegranate Artbooks/The British Library, San Francisco/London, 1997

De Hamel, Christopher: 'The Gutenberg Bible', chapter in *The Book. A History of the Bible*, Phaidon, London, 2001

Fletcher, H George: Gutenberg and the Genesis of Printing, The Pierpont Morgan Library, New York, 1994

Hellinga, Lotte: 'Johann Fust, Peter Schoeffer, and Nicolas Jenson', article in *Gutenberg Jahrbuch*, Mainz, 2003

Hellinga, Lotte: *William Caxton and Early Printing in England*, The British Library, London, 2010

Stillwell, Margaret Bingham: *The Beginning of the World of Books, 1450 to 1470*, The Bibliographical Society of America, New York, 1972

Wagner, Bettina: *Als die Lettern laufen lernten. Inkunabeln aus der Bayerischen Staatsbibliothek München*, Reichert Verlag, Wiesbaden, 2009

Italian Renaissance Types

Barker, Nicolas: 'The Aldine Italic', article in *A Millennium of the Book, production, design, and illustration in manuscript and print, 900–1900*, ed. Robin Myers and Michael Harris, Oak Knoll Press, New Castle, 1995

Davies, Martin: *Aldus Manutius, printer and publisher of renaissance Venice*, J Paul Getty Museum/The British Library, Malibu/London, 1995

Ehrle, Francis and Paul Liebaert: *Specimina Codicum Latinorum Vaticanorum*, Walter de Gruyter, Berlin and Leipzig, 1932

Fletcher, H George: *In Praise of Aldus Manutius, a quincentenary exhibition*, The Pierpont Morgan Library, New York, 1995

Lowry, Martin: *The World of Aldus Manutius*, Basil Blackwell, Oxford, 1979

Lowry, Martin with George Abrams: *Venetian Printing*, Poul Kristensen, Herning, 1989

Lowry, Martin: *Nicolas Jenson and the rise of Venetian publishing in renaissance Europe*, Basil Blackwell, Oxford, 1991

Morison, Stanley: 'Early Humanistic Script and the First Roman Type', article in *The Library*, Fourth Series, volume XXIV, numbers 1 and 2, Oxford, June and September 1943

Olocco, Riccardo: *De Littera Veneta, breve trattato sul carattere inciso per il De Aetna di Pietro Bembo a confronto con revival storici del XX secolo*, Inside Editore, Bolzano, 2010

Osley, Arthur S: 'The Origins of Italic Type', article in *Calligraphy and Palaeography*, ed. A S Osley, Faber & Faber, London, 1965

French Renaissance Types

Amert, Kay: *The Scythe and the Rabbit, Simon de Colines and the culture of the book in renaissance Paris*, ed. Robert Bringhurst, Cary Graphic Arts Press, Rochester, 2012

Barker, Nicolas: 'The Aldine Roman in Paris', article in *The Library*, ed. John Dreyfus and Peter Davison, Fifth Series, volume XXIX, number 1, Oxford, March 1974

Johnson, A F: 'The Chancery Types of Italy and France', 1924 article in *Selected Essays on Books and Printing*, ed. Percy H Muir, Van Gendt & Co / Routledge & Kegan Paul / Abner Schram, Amsterdam / London / New York, 1970

Johnson, A F: 'The Italic Types of Robert Granjon', 1941 article in *Selected Essays on Books and Printing*, ed. Percy H Muir, Van Gendt & Co / Routledge & Kegan Paul / Abner Schram, Amsterdam / London / New York, 1970

Mosley, James: 'Garamond, Griffo and Others, the price of celebrity', article in *Bibliologia*, Istituti Editoriali e Poligrafici Internazionali, Pisa and Rome, 1, 2006

Parent, Annie and Jeanne Veyrin-Forrer: 'Claude Garamont, new documents', article in *The Library*, ed. John Dreyfus and Peter Davison, Fifth Series, volume XXIX, number 1, Oxford, March 1974

Schreiber, Fred: *Simon de Colines, an annotated catalogue of 230 examples of his press, 1520-1546*, intro by Jeanne Veyrin-Forrer, Friends of Brigham Young University, Provo, 1995

Vervliet, Hendrik D L: 'The Garamond Types of Christopher Plantin', article in the *Journal of the Printing Historical Society*, ed. James Mosley, London, number 1, 1965

Vervliet, Hendrik D L: *The Palaeotypography of the French Renaissance*, 2 volumes, Brill, Leiden and Boston, 2008

Vervliet, Hendrik D L: *French Renaissance Printing Types, a Conspectus*, Oak Knoll Press / The Bibliographical Society / The Printing Historical Society, New Castle / London / London, 2010

Baroque Types

Beaujon, Paul [Beatrice Warde]: 'The "Garamond" Types, XVI and XVII century sources considered', article in *The Fleuron*, volume V, ed. Stanley Morison, London, 1926

Beaujon, Paul [Beatrice Warde]: *The 1621 Specimen of Jean Jannon, Paris & Sedan, designer and engraver of the caractères de l'Université now owned by the Imprimerie Nationale*, in facsimile, Librairie Ancienne Honoré Champion, Paris, 1927

Buday, George: 'Some more Notes on Nicolas Kis of the "Janson" Types', article in *The Library*, ed. John Dreyfus and Peter Davison, Fifth Series, volume XXIX, number 1, Oxford, March 1974

Carter, Harry and George Buday: 'The Origin of the Janson Types, with a note on Nicolas Kis', article in *Linotype Matrix*, number 18, London, 1954

Carter, Harry and George Buday: 'Nicolas Kis and the Janson Types', article in *Gutenberg Jahrbuch*, Mainz, 1957

Carter, Harry: 'Caslon Punches, an Interim Note', article in the *Journal of the Printing Historical Society*, ed. James Mosley, London, number 1, 1965

Dodson, Alan: 'A Type for All Seasons', article in *Type & Typography, highlights from* Matrix, *the review for printers and bibliophiles*, intro John Randle and John D Berry, Mark Batty Publisher, New York, 2003

Haiman, György: *Nicolas Kis, a Hungarian punch-cutter and printer, 1650–1702*, Jack W Stauffacher / The Greenwood Press, San Francisco, 1983

Heiderhoff, Horst: 'The Rediscovery of a Type designer: Miklós Kis', article in *Fine Print on Type*, ed. Charles Bigelow, Paul Hayden Duensing, and Linnea Gentry, Bedford Arts, San Francisco, 1989

Howes, Justin: 'The Compleat Caslon', article in *Type & Typography, highlights from* Matrix, *the review for printers and bibliophiles*, intro John Randle and John D Berry, Mark Batty Publisher, New York, 2003

Johnson, A F: 'The Goût Hollandois', article in *The Library*, Fourth Series, volume XX, number 2, London, 1939

Lane, John A: *Early Type Specimens in the Plantin-Moretus Museum*, preface by Hendrik D L Vervliet, Oak Knoll Press / The British Library, New Castle / London, 2004

Middendorp, Jan: *Dutch Type*, 010 Publishers, Rotterdam, 2004

Mosley, James: 'The Early Career of William Caslon', article in the *Journal of the Printing Historical Society*, ed. James Mosley, London, number 3, 1967

Mosley, James: 'A Specimen of Printing Types by William Caslon, London 1766', in facsimile in the *Journal of the Printing Historical Society*, ed. James Mosley, London, number 16, 1983

Paillard, Jean: *Claude Garamont, graveur et fondeur de lettres*, M Ollière & Co, Paris, 1914

Parker, Mike: 'Early Typefounders' Moulds at the Plantin-Moretus Museum', article in *The Library*, ed. John Dreyfus and Peter Davison, Fifth Series, volume XXIX, number 1, Oxford, March 1974

Neoclassical Types

Benton, Josiah Henry: *John Baskerville, typefounder and printer, 1706–1775*, Burt Franklin, New York, 1968

Chambers, David: *Caractères de l'Imprimerie, nouvelles Gravés par S P Fournier le jeune* (1742), in facsimile, St Bride Printing Library Museum, 1975

Dreyfus, John: 'The Baskerville Punches, 1750–1950', article in *The Library*, Fifth Series, volume V, number 1, Oxford, 1950

Hutt, Allen: *Fournier, the compleat typographer*, Frederick Muller, London, 1972

Jammes, André: 'Académisme et Typographie, the making of the romain du roi', article in the *Journal of the Printing Historical Society*, ed. James Mosley, London, no. 1, 1965

Middendorp, Jan: *Dutch Type*, 010 Publishers, Rotterdam, 2004

Mosley, James: 'French Academicians and Modern Typography, designing new types in the 1690s', article in *Typography Papers*, number 2, Reading University, Department of Typography and Graphic Communication, Reading, 1997

Mosley, James: 'Les Caractères de l'Imprimerie Royale', chapter in *Le Romain du Roi, la typographie au service de l'Etat, 1702–2002*, Musée de l'imprimerie, Lyon, 2002

Mosley, James: 'Médailles sur les principaux événements du règne de Louis le Grand, 1702. The making of the book', article in *Bulletin du Bibliophile*, Paris, number 2, 2008

Mosley, James: 'The Romain du Roi, a type made for the royal printing-house of Louis XIV', chapter in *Printing for Kingdom, Empire, and Republic, treasures from the archives of the Imprimerie nationale*, ed. H George Fletcher, The Grolier Club, New York, 2011

Pardoe, F E: *John Baskerville of Birmingham, letter-founder and printer*, Frederick Muller, London, 1975

Rational Types

Didot, Pierre: *Épitre sur les progrés de l'imprimerie*, chez Didot l'aîné, Paris, 1784

Ewald, Friedrich: 'The Officina Bodoni' article in *The Fleuron*, volume VII, ed. Stanley Morison, London, 1930

Füssel, Stephan: *Manual of Typography, Giambattista Bodoni, Manuale Tipografico,* (1818) in facsimile, Taschen, Cologne, 2010

George, Alfred J: *The Didot Family and the progress of printing*, Syracuse University Press, Syracuse, 1961

Lane, John A: *Early Type Specimens in the Plantin-Moretus Museum*, preface by Hendrik D L Vervliet, Oak Knoll Press/The British Library, New Castle/London, 2004

Nineteenth-century Types

Bruce, David Jr: *History of Typefounding in the United States* (1874), reprint, The Typophiles, New York, 1981

Freeman, Janet Ing: 'Founders' Type and Private Founts at the Chiswick Press in the 1850s', article in the *Journal of the Printing Historical Society*, ed. James Mosley, number 19 and 20, London, 1985 to 1987

Gray, Nicolete: 'Slab-serif design in England, 1815–1845, article in the *Journal of the Printing Historical Society*, ed. James Mosley, number 15, London, 1980/81

Johnson, A F: 'The Modern-face Type in England', 1932 article in *Selected Essays on Books and Printing*, ed. Percy H Muir, Van Gendt & Co/Routledge & Kegan Paul/Abner Schram, Amsterdam/London/New York, 1970

Johnson, A F: 'English Type Specimen Books', 1933 article in *Selected Essays on Books and Printing*, ed. Percy H Muir, Van Gendt & Co/Routledge & Kegan Paul/Abner Schram, Amsterdam/London/New York, 1970

Johnston, Alastair M: *Alphabets to Order, the literature of nineteenth-century typefounders' specimens*, Oak Knoll Press/The British Library, New Castle/London, 2000

Johnston, Alastair M: *Transitional Faces, the lives and work of Richard Austin, type-cutter, and Richard Turner Austin, wood-engraver*, (forthcoming)

Loy, William E: *Nineteenth-century American Designers and Engravers of Type*, ed. Alastair M Johnston and Stephen O Saxe, Oak Knoll Press, New Castle, 2009

Mosley, James: '"Scotch Roman", what it is and how it got its name', article in *The Ampersand*, volume 17, number 3/4, Pacific Center for the Book Arts, San Francisco, Autumn/Winter 1998

Mosley, James: *The Nymph and the Grot, the revival of the sanserif letter*, Friends of the St Bride Printing Library, London, 1999

Reed, Talbot Baines: *The History of the Old English Letter Foundries*, ed. A F Johnson, Faber and Faber, London, 1952

Twyman, Michael: 'The Bold Idea, the Use of Bold-looking Types in the Nineteenth Century', article in the *Journal of the Printing Historical Society*, ed. James Mosley, number 22, London, 1993

Private Press Types

Dreyfus, John: 'New Light on the Design of Types for the Kelmscott and Doves Presses', article in *The Library*, ed. John Dreyfus and Peter Davison, Fifth Series, volume XXIX, number 1, Oxford, March 1974

Franklin, Colin: *The Private Presses*, Dufour Editions, Chester Springs, 1969

MacCarthy, Fiona: *William Morris, a life for our times*, Alfred A Knoff/Faber and Faber, New York/London, 1995

Newdigate, Bernard H: 'Mr C H St John Hornby's Ashendene Press', article in *The Fleuron*, volume II, ed. Oliver Simon, London, 1924

Newdigate, Bernard H: 'Emery Walker', article in *The Fleuron*, volume IV, ed. Oliver Simon, London, 1925

Peterson, William S: 'The Type-designs of William Morris', article in the *Journal of the Printing Historical Society*, ed. James Mosley, number 19 and 20, London, 1985 to 1987

Peterson, William S: *The Kelmscott Press, a history of William Morris's typographic adventure*, University of California Press/Oxford University Press, Berkeley/Oxford, 1991

Tidcombe, Marianne: *The Doves Press*, Oak Knoll Press/The British Library, New Castle/London, 2002

Warde, Beatrice: 'A Descriptive Bibliography of the Books Printed at the Ashendene Press', article in *Signature*, number 1, London, 1935

Online resources

Boardley, John: Website, I Love Typography. http://ilovetypography.com

Mosley, James: Blog, Typefoundry. http://typefoundry.blogspot.com

Indices

Index of Names

Agüera y Arcas, Blaise   10
Arnisbergh, Frederica   15
Arnisbergh, Georgius de   15
Arrighi, Ludovico degli   35, 71
Augereau, Antoine   9, 39, 43
Austin, Richard   83
Barbarigo, Pierfrancesco   29
Baldasso, Renzo   23
Barbé, Jean   13
Baskerville, John   8, 65, 73, 75, 79
Baskerville, Sarah   75
Beaujon, Paul [Beatrice Warde]   41, 49
Bell, John   83
Bembo, Pietro   29
Benton, Linn Boyd   8
Besley, Robert   85, 89
Biagiarelli, Berta Maracchi   57
Bignon, Jean-Paul   13, 65
Bí Sheng   13
Boardley, John   23
Bodoni, Giambattista   9, 65, 67, 69, 77, 79, 81, 83
Bodoni, Margherita   81
Bowyer, William   61, 63
Brown, Michelle   47
Bruce, David Jr   8, 87
Bruce, George   9, 87
Buday, George   59
Burgundy, Margaret Duchess of   21
Calvin, John   51
Carter, Harry   9, 59, 71
Caslon, Elizabeth   63
Caslon, William I   61, 63, 87
Caslon, William II   63
Caslon, William III   63
Caslon, William IV   9
Caxton, William   21
Cecchi, Giovanni Filippo   57, 59
Chappell, Warren   8, 55
Charles V   35
Charles VII   10
Claesz, Hendrik   53
Cobden, Annie   91
Cobden-Sanderson, Thomas James   89, 91
Cockerell, Sydney Carlyle   93
Colines, Simon de   9, 37, 39
Constantin, 'Maître'   39
Conway, Melissa   10
Corvinum, George   45
Cousin, Jean   47
Cramoisy, Sébastien   49
Des Billettes, Gilles Filleau   65
De Vinne, Theodore L   10
Dickinson, Samuel   83, 87
Diderot, Denis   71
Didot, Firmin   65, 67, 69, 77, 79, 83
Didot, François-Ambroise   13, 77

Didot, Pierre   77
Duchâtel, Pierre   43
Elsevier, Daniel   53, 55, 57
Enschedé, Charles   67
Enschedé, Izaak   67
Enschedé, Johann   67
Estienne, Henri   37
Estienne, Robert I   29, 37, 39, 41, 43, 49
Figgins, Vincent   85
Fleischman, Johann   8, 9, 67
Fournier, Jean-Claude   69
Fournier, Jean-Pierre   69
Fournier, Pierre-Simon   13, 65, 69, 71, 81
Fox, Benjamin   85
François I   39, 43
Fust, Johann   19
Garamont, Claude   9, 13, 37, 39, 41, 43, 45, 49, 51, 55, 57, 65, 69, 87
Gagny, Jean de   41
Ged, William   61
Grandison, William   87
Grandjean, Philippe   13, 65
Granjon, Robert   9, 41, 43, 45, 47, 51, 55
Griffo, Francesco   29, 31, 33, 35, 71
Gutenberg, Johann   8, 9, 10, 11, 12, 15, 17, 27
Haiman, György   59
Handy, John   75
Hansard, T C   83
Haultin, Pierre   8
Hellinga, Lotte   10
Hewitt, Graily   91, 93
Hornby, Charles Henry St John   93
Jannon, Jean   9, 41, 49, 51
Janson, Anton   59
Jaugeon, Jacques   65
Jenson, Nicolas   10, 23, 25, 27, 29, 37, 65, 89, 91
Johnston, Alastair   83
Johnston, Edward   91
Keates, C E   91
Kis, Miklós Tótfalusi   57, 59
Lange, Robert   21
Lear, Edward   8
Le Bé, Guillaume I   43
Le Bé Guillaume II   37, 39, 43
Louis XIII   51
Louis XIV   65
Loy, William E   87
Luther, Martin   51
Mansion, Colard   21
Manutius, Aldus   9, 29, 31, 33, 35, 39, 65, 69, 87
Mardersteig, Giovanni   29, 31
Martin, Henri-Jean   9
Medici, Giulio de'   35
Miller, William   8, 87
Molnár, József   59
Moncenigo, Giovanni   23
Morison, Stanley   9, 25, 45, 55, 89, 93

Morris, William   89, 91, 93
Mosley, James   9, 13, 49, 61
Moxon, Joseph   13
Müller, Johann   23
Needham, Paul   10
Néobar, Conrad   39
Olocco, Riccardo   31
Orsi, Luigi   81
Osley, Arthur S   35
Paciaudi, Paolo Maria   79
Paillard, Jean   49
Palmer, Samuel   61
Pannartz, Arnold   25, 93
Pardoe, F E   73
Parma, Duke of   79, 81
Perugino, Lautizio   35
Petrarch, Francesco   25
Phemister, Alexander   9, 87
Phillips, John   83
Pickering, William   61
Plantin, Christophe   13, 45
Pollard, A W   91
Porson, Richard   83
Prince, Edward   89, 91, 93
Racine, Jean   77
Ratdolt, Erhard   9, 23
Reed, Talbot Baines   85
Richelieu, Cardinal duc de   49, 51
Royer, Jean le   47
Rubeus, Jacobus   89
San Vito, Bartolomeo   47
Schoeffer, Peter   17, 19, 25
Silvius, Willem   45
Simonneau, Louis   65
Singrener, Johann   47
Slimbach, Robert   41
Smith, John   13
Soncino, Gershom   33
Sweynheym, Konrad   25, 93
Thorowgood, William   85
Tiffin, Percy   91
Tillot, Guglielmo du   79
Torresani, Andrea   29
Trissino, Gian Giorgio   35
Truchet, Sébastien   13, 65, 71
Twyman, Michael   85
Updike, Daniel Berkeley   9, 51
Van den Keere, Hendrik   9
Van Dijck, Abraham   53
Van Dijck, Christoffel   53, 55
Vascosan, Michel de   41, 43, 47
Veldener, Johan   21
Vervliet, Hendrik   13, 37, 39, 43, 45, 47
Viart, Guyonne   37
Von Speyer, Johann   27
Voskens, Dirck   57, 61
Walker, Emery   89, 91, 93

Warde, Beatrice   9, 41, 49, 51
Wagner, Bettina   23
Whittingham, Charles   61, 63
Wilson, Alexander   83
Zell, Ulrich   21

Index of Places

Amsterdam   53, 55, 57, 59, 67
Antwerp   45
Ashendene   93
Augsburg   23
Auxerre   69
Bassiano   29
Birmingham   73, 75
Bologna   33
Boston   83, 87
Bruges   21
Budapest   59
Caen   51
Cambridge   53, 55, 83
Chelsea   93
Cologne   15, 21, 25
Dexheim   53
Edinburgh   83, 87
Exeter   85
Fano   33
Ferrara   29
Florence   10, 57, 59
Frankenthal   53
Frankfurt   27, 45, 59, 67
Geneva   45
Gernsheim   19
Ghent   21
Glasgow   83
Haarlem   55, 67
Hales Owen   61
Hague, The   67
Hammersmith   89, 91
Kidderminster   75
Kolozsvár   59
Leipzig   57
London   21, 61, 63, 77, 83, 85
Lyons   45
Mainz   10, 11, 15, 17, 19, 21, 25, 27
New Jersey   8
New York   9, 87
Nuremberg   23, 67
Oppenheim   53
Oxford   45
Padua   47
Paris   17, 19, 37, 39, 41, 43, 45, 47, 49, 51, 65, 69, 71, 77, 79, 81
Parma   79, 81
Ripoli   10
Rome   25, 29, 31, 35, 45, 79
Saluzzo   79
Sedan   49, 51

Sommevoire   27
Stockholm   45
Subiaco   25, 93
Tours   27
Venice   23, 27, 29, 31, 35, 39, 41
Vienna   47
Weald of Kent   21
Westminster   21
Wolverly   75

Index of Call Numbers

BERN
   Universitätsbibliothek Bern
      ZB Bong I 25:7   36

CAMBRIDGE
   University Library
      UL I*.7 .3-4 (A)   44

CHICAGO
   The Newberry Library
      Case f 3919 .314   38
      Case y 642 .0635   42
      Case Wing z 40539 .311   68, 70
      Case Wing z 40543 .9722   82
      Case Wing z 40546 .2642   2, 66
      Inc. 3288   24
      Inc. 4064   26
      Inc. 4383   22
      Inc. 5550   28
      Wing z 40543 .5733   86
      Wing z 40545 .093   84
      Wing z 40583 .1245   10
      Wing zp 535 .l965   34
      Wing zp 535 .s7023   32
      Wing zp 539 .l565   46
      Wing zp 539 .v478   40
      Wing zp 639 .p208   50
      Wing zp 735 .b627   78, 80
      Wing zp 739 .d563   76
      Wing zp 739 .p212   64
      Wing zp 745 .b30646   72, 74
      Wing zp 745 .c14   52, 54
      Wing zp 845 .c4375   60
      Wing zp845 .k336   88
      Wing zp 845 .w613   62
      Wing zp 945 .a822   92
      Wing zp 945 .d7408   90

MANCHESTER
   The John Rylands Library, The University of Manchester
      JRL 3069   16
      JRL 3103   12
      JRL 9784   Front cover, 18
      JRL 11567   20
      JRL 17250.1   14

PARIS
   Bibliothèque Mazarine
      A.15226 (2)   48

PARMA
   Biblioteca Palatina
      LL VII 8   30

URBANA-CHAMPAIGN
   University of Illinois, The Rare Book and Manuscript Library
      IUQ00233   56, 58

WASHINGTON
   Library of Congress
      Ms 8   11

COLOPHON

Book design by Stan Knight
Typography and pre-press by Marcia Friedman

The text face is 10½ on 12 Adobe Garamond Pro
with Adobe Garamond Premier Pro glyphs
all designed by Robert Slimbach